Your Aquarium Here

Your Aquarium Here

The author can be reached at:

Mastery Academy of Chinese Metaphysics Sdn. Bhd. (611143-A)
19-3, The Boulevard, Mid Valley City,
59200 Kuala Lumpur, Malaysia.
Tel   : +603-2284 8080
Fax   : +603-2284 1218
Email   : info@masteryacademy.com
Website: www.masteryacademy.com

DISCLAIMER:

The author, Joey Yap and the publisher, JY Books Sdn Bhd, have made their best efforts to produce this high quality, informative and helpful book. They have verified the technical accuracy of the information and contents of this book. Any information pertaining to the events, occurrences, dates and other details relating to the person or persons, dead or alive, and to the companies have been verified to the best of their abilities based on information obtained or extracted from various websites, newspaper clippings and other public media. However, they make no representation or warranties of any kind with regard to the contents of this book and accept no liability of any kind for any losses or damages caused or alleged to be caused directly or indirectly from using the information contained herein.

Published by JY Books Sdn. Bhd. (659134-T)

Table of Contents

Preface

As a writer of classical Feng Shui books, I have the great advantage of often hearing near instantaneous feedback about my work through my work as a trainer, public speaker and consultant. It has been gratifying for me to know that my writing has helped many people explore and understand the world of Chinese Metaphysics, and subjects like Feng Shui, BaZi and Face Reading. These subjects were until recently, off-limits to those who could not read Chinese. Frankly, even those who can read Chinese would have found the subject daunting given the volume of content on this subject that is available, and the near impossible task of separating the wheat from the chaff.

Two of my books changed my perspective and approach towards writing books on Feng Shui, and also to some degree, have influenced my approach towards the teaching of classical Feng Shui. When I wrote the 'Feng Shui for Homebuyers', I had reservations about boiling the subject down to such a simple level. Not because the subject doesn't lend itself towards simplification, but that it would then be difficult to distinguish classical Feng Shui techniques, from New Age Feng Shui techniques.

In writing 'Feng Shui for Homebuyers', I realised that I needed to provide the practical information that a layperson needs to make their decision or help guide their decision. But at the same time, I had to make sure there was adequate and appropriate technical information so that they could understand what they were putting into practice. Most importantly, they would be able to appreciate that the principles they were utilising were authentic and supported by classical Feng Shui theory as found in the classics.

The overwhelming public response to the Homebuyers series, and the subsequent feedback I received from the public on those books, prompted me to re-consider writing what I have always considered to be 'simplified' books (and I might add, thinner books, as some readers confessed they found my books rather voluminous and somewhat intimidating!) As a trainer, and consultant, there is always a hesitance about simplification. It is a bit of a double-edged sword – whilst it creates a high level of accessibility and enables more people to benefit from Feng Shui, it also means the results are a bit more generalised because the solution has not be tailored to the person or the house.

But I also appreciate, after talking to many readers of the Homebuyers series at my public events and talks, and also, interacting with the students in my new *Feng Shui for Life* course, that not everyone has the aptitude, inclination or affinity towards Feng Shui and studying Feng Shui. Yet that should not mean they are precluded from utilising it, especially if they feel they cannot afford a consultant or for some reason, do not think the cost of a consultant is warranted.

So was born my 'Fengshuilogy' series of books.

This is a series of highly practical Feng Shui books, designed for the person who wants to be able to do fuss-free Feng Shui. It requires minimal understanding and Feng Shui knowledge to implement. All you will need to do is take the Facing Direction of your home. Then turn to the page which relates to your property's Facing Direction and you will find a Flying Star chart, with all the relevant information already marked out for you. All you need to do is TAKE ACTION.

Your Aquarium Here is the first of the Fengshuilogy series and I chose the subject of aquariums for several reasons. Firstly, the placement of an aquarium or water feature is one of the most common techniques used by Flying Star Feng Shui practitioners to activate Qi in a property. Secondly, aquariums can be used in both landed property and high-rise property without too much trouble. And thirdly, it is a Feng Shui technique which is generally well within the realms of public knowledge.

In line with ensuring there is a balance of technical information and also, to ensure more advanced users of Feng Shui also get a benefit from reading this book, I have included a commentary section in each Flying Star chart. You will also find a comprehensive introduction to the use of Water in Classical Feng Shui, and technical information such as the types of Water, the classification of Water, Water Forms and some debunking of the renowned myths about how water is used within Classical Feng Shui. Skip this part if you're more a practical person who just wants to know the basic information. But if you're also curious to understand the hows and whys, some answers are also present.

Good luck and have fun!

Warmest regards,

Joey Yap
San Francisco, August, 2008

Author's personal website: www.joeyyap.com | www.fengshuilogy.com (Personal blog)
Academy website: www.masteryacademy.com | www.masteryjournal.com | www.maelearning.com

MASTERY ACADEMY
OF CHINESE METAPHYSICS™

At **www.masteryacademy.com**, you will find some useful tools to ascertain key information about the Feng Shui of a property or for the study of Astrology.

The Joey Yap Flying Stars Calculator can be utilised to plot your home or office Flying Stars chart. To find out your personal best directions, use the 8 Mansions Calculator. To learn more about your personal Destiny, you can use the Joey Yap BaZi Ming Pan Calculator to plot your Four Pillars of Destiny – you just need to have your date of birth (day, month, year) and time of birth.

For more information about BaZi, Xuan Kong or Flying Star Feng Shui, or if you wish to learn more about these subjects with Joey Yap, logon to the Mastery Academy of Chinese Metaphysics website at **www.masteryacademy.com.**

MASTERY ACADEMY
E-LEARNING CENTER
www.maelearning.com

www.maelearning.com

Bookmark this address on your computer, and visit this newly-launched website today. With the E-Learning Center, knowledge of Chinese Metaphysics is a mere 'click' away!

Our E-Learning Center consists of 3 distinct components.

1. Online Courses

These shall comprise of 3 Programs: our Online Feng Shui Program, Online BaZi Program, and Online Mian Xiang Program. Each lesson contains a video lecture, slide presentation and downloadable course notes.

2. MA Live!

With MA Live!, Joey Yap's workshops, tutorials, courses and seminars on various Chinese Metaphysics subjects broadcasted right to your computer screen. Better still, participants will not only get to see and hear Joey talk 'live', but also get to engage themselves directly in the event and more importantly, TALK to Joey via the MA Live! interface. All the benefits of a live class, minus the hassle of actually having to attend one!

3. Video-On-Demand (VOD)

Get immediate streaming-downloads of the Mastery Academy's wide range of educational DVDs, right on your computer screen. No more shipping costs and waiting time to be incurred!

Study at your own pace, and interact with your Instructor and fellow students worldwide… at your own convenience and privacy. With our E-Learning Center, knowledge of Chinese Metaphysics is brought DIRECTLY to you in all its clarity, with illustrated presentations and comprehensive notes expediting your learning curve!

Welcome to the Mastery Academy's E-LEARNING CENTER…YOUR virtual gateway to Chinese Metaphysics mastery!

BEFORE YOU START

This book has been designed to be as simple and easy to use as possible. In fact, you could just skip straight to Chapter 4 if you're simply looking for a fuss-free approach to deploying Classical Feng Shui in your home. Whilst I feel that understanding is always preferred over mere application, I do understand that not everyone has the inclination or interest in learning about Feng Shui, but has an interest in making use of Feng Shui to gain an advantage. So if you are the practical 'get to the point' sort, skip straight to Chapter 4. If however you are a little interested in the whys and hows, then read on.

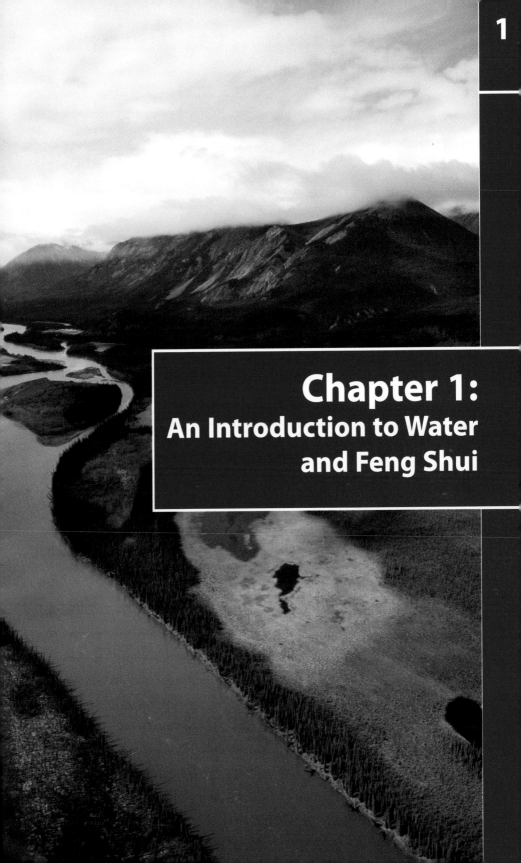

Chapter 1:
An Introduction to Water and Feng Shui

An Introduction to Water and Feng Shui

How's this for a simple idea. Feng Shui, literally translated, is Wind Water. So, logically, that would mean, Feng Shui is centered around two things: Wind and Water. And that Water is one half of the system that makes up Feng Shui. So if something in Feng Shui revolves around Water, it must by necessity be powerful, potent and half of what constitutes Feng Shui.

It is true that Water, as an element, is an extremely important aspect of Chinese Metaphysics. It is one of the Five Elements, and one of the Five Elements that is regarded as essential. In the study of BaZi, Water, together with Fire, are regarded as two of the key elements that every BaZi chart must have. In Feng Shui, Water is an important tool and component of Feng Shui. But that is NOT because it is one half of the name.

I might add, there are no Wind Formulas in Feng Shui.

In Feng Shui and to a larger degree Metaphysics, everything comes down to the basic principle of Yin and Yang, and the concept of Balance between Yin and Yang. In Metaphysics, we are searching for the perfection in duality. The significance of Water in Feng Shui is related to its Yang quality. So it is not wrong to say it is one half of the equation, but this is due to its fulfilling one part of the equation of Yin and Yang, rather than simply because one of the two words in 'Feng Shui' is Water.

What IS the role of Water in Feng Shui?

乘風則散，界水則止
Qi is dispersed by the Wind and gathers at the boundaries of Water.

This singular line from the foremost classics on Feng Shui, the Burial Book, instantly defines the role of Water in Feng Shui. As Qi gathers where Water is found, Water plays the role of accumulating, collecting and gathering Qi. Where there is Water, is where the Qi stops. And when Qi stops, it collects and accumulates. In the same vein, Water can also be used to barricade, direct and re-direct, as well as to retain or hold in Sheng Qi and diffuse or neutralise Sha Qi appropriately.

As the Yang component or active component in Feng Shui, Water's role naturally also relates to activation or movement. The role of Water in Feng Shui therefore is to activate, circulate and move the Qi.

In itself, Water does not emit Qi. Only Mountains, the Yin component of Feng Shui, produce and emit Qi. And lest we forget, Wind has a significance in Feng Shui too. Thus, Mountains produce the Qi, the Wind carries the Qi down the Mountains, and the Water collects, activates and gives impetus to the Qi.

Mountains produce Qi, Wind transports Qi, and Water activates Qi. This is one way to sum up Feng Shui.

Thus, Water is needed to enable the Qi of an area to become usable and active. Water is used to control the Qi movement by focusing or directing it since Water can barricade Qi. Sometimes, Water is used to force Qi to gather at certain points, deemed appropriate by the Feng Shui consultant based on certain principles and tenets of Feng Shui.

In essence, Water is needed to bring to life the Feng Shui of an area borne out of the mountains and landforms. Hence, placing or using Water is one of the most common prescriptions afforded by most Feng Shui masters in the course of a Feng Shui audit. An area could have perfect landform, or superb Qi, but without Water, it is untapped potential.

Mountains produce Qi, Wind transports Qi, and Water activates Qi. This is one way to sum up Feng Shui.

The Ways of Water

Whilst there are also Formulas which make use of Mountain Formations, and which emphasise the Mountains rather than the Water (focusing in Yin rather than Yang as it were), these are somewhat unpopular in the instant gratification world we live in today. Mountain Formulas of course have their role – if one were designing a national capital, or perhaps a large structure like a stadium, a housing estate or a gated community, these formulas would typically come into play. But predominantly Water  (and accordingly Water Formulas) is the favoured tool of the Feng Shui master because it is not only an activating force, but because Water generally also produces quicker and more immediate results.

Water is also easy to deploy – it can be used with or without the need for renovation or alterations, and in select instances where the prescription goes down to the exact degree, it is not required in large bodies or quantities. As such, Water is a versatile tool in the tool box of the Feng Shui consultant. It can be the first choice of the Feng Shui consultant, or the last line of defence.

Water is a versatile tool in the tool box of the Feng Shui consultant.

The speed of the results and the extent of the outcome depend of course on the type of Water Formula used. San Yuan Water methods tend to have faster results than San He's Water methods. This is because San Yuan focuses its calculations on Qi flow, whilst San He starts from the Forms. But the bottom line is that Water is the preferred option when speed is required (usually most of the time!)

There are many systems and methods for using Water in Feng Shui. There are also many different types of Water – Internal Water, External Water, Virtual Water, Natural Water, Man-Made Water. There are even different Natural Water Formations. The subject of Water is itself is an extremely broad subject, which cannot really be fully explained or explored in a singular text. Indeed, there are many classical texts on this subject, each covering a different area of understanding and application. Classical texts such as *Di Li Wu Jue* 地理五訣 *(Earthly Principles Five Verses)*, *Ru Di Yan* 入地眼 *(Entering Earth Eye)*, *Shui Long Jing* 水龍經 *(Water Dragon Classics)* and *Xue Xin Fu* 雪心賦 *(Snow Heart Classics)* are some of the key sources for theories and principles relating to Water Feng Shui.

There are also many different types of Water – Internal Water, External Water, Virtual Water, Natural Water, Man-Made Water.

However, in the course of Chapter 2, my goal is to help you gain a better understanding of this vital, yet frequently misused, component of Feng Shui. Whilst you may not have a total grasp of how Water is used in Feng Shui, by the end of this book, you certainly will have a better idea of at least, how it SHOULD NOT be used, and how to avoid the common mistakes that people make when it comes to utilising Water for Feng Shui purposes. And of course, you will be able to ascertain a suitable location for Water in your own home.

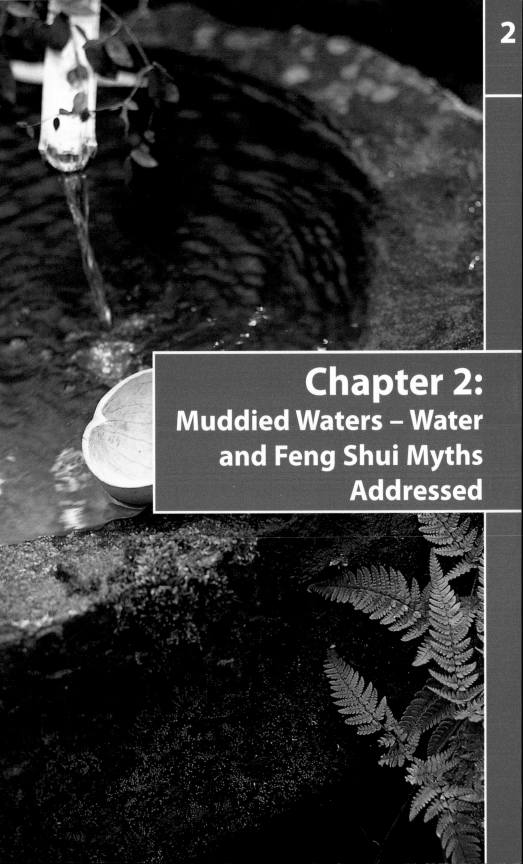

Chapter 2:
Muddied Waters – Water and Feng Shui Myths Addressed

Muddied Waters – Water and Feng Shui Myths Addressed

I want to clear some of the misconceptions, false expectations and old wives tales out of the way before I go into more depth about how Water is used in classical Feng Shui.

Water Myth #1:
Water = Wealth.

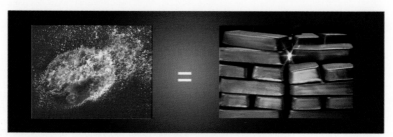

You may have heard of the Chinese saying '水爲財'. The literal English translation is Water IS Money or Water equals Money. In Cantonese slang, the word 'water' is also often used to refer to 'money'. Thus, it is from here perhaps that the Feng Shui myths that Water has a direct co-relation with Wealth, or that water represents livelihood or water symbolizes wealth flowing into the house, originated. An extreme version of the myth actually holds that water (any water) means wealth and the more water the house has around it and inside, the more wealth the occupants will experience or have. This myth may also have grown out of the Feng Shui saying: 'Water governs Wealth, Mountains Govern People'.

In reality, this saying does not actually mean Water = Money. Many Feng Shui sayings tend to have hidden or coded meanings, which disguise the actual point being made. The reference to "Water" in this saying is not meant to be literal, but refers to Yang activities. In classical Feng Shui, Water is regarded as the foremost representation of the Yang element.

The fact is that Water in itself, does not symbolize, equate with, or directly refer to wealth. Water does not in itself create, attract or generate wealth in the sense of dollars and cents.

Water is simply an activator in Feng Shui and amongst one of the aspects that Water can have a positive effect on is wealth. But it can also be used to activate Qi to improve health, to help speed up recuperation from a health problem, to improve relationships, to resolve conflicts, to assist couples who wish to conceive, or to simply improve harmony in the household.

Since Water is only an ACTIVATOR, what it activates, and the outcomes it produces depends on what Qi (in the form of what Flying Star for example) is located in the area where Water is located. So it is erroneous to say that Water Feng Shui is the key to great wealth or getting rich. Water Feng Shui can also be the key to good health, harmonious relationships or finding the love of your life.

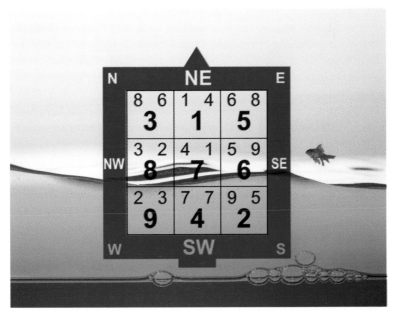

Since Water is only an ACTIVATOR, what it activates, and the outcomes it produces depends on what Qi (in the form of what Flying Star for example) is located in the area where Water is located.

Water Myth #2:
Faux Water Dragons vs the real
Water Dragon.

Many English language books on Water Feng Shui use the term 'Water Dragons' to give a mythic dimension to the concept of Water Feng Shui that they are espousing. They probably have to do this because what they are doing in effect is recommending the building or construction of drains, or visible drainage (such as open gutters) systems. "Water Dragon" sounds much more potent, powerful, and awe-inspiring than 'Drain'. And "Water Feng Shui" certainly sounds a lot more inspiring than "Drain Water Feng Shui".

The reality is that you are not constructing any kind of Water Dragon. In classical Feng Shui, the term 'Water Dragon' comes from a book called the *Water Dragon Classics* 水龍經. The *Water Dragon Classics* is a book about Flatland Dragons or how to read landforms when the land is absolutely flat. In such situations, water formations are treated as if they are mountains (which are the true Dragons in Feng Shui), and practitioners are supposed to look at the water, as if it were a mountain formation. Hence the term 'Water Dragons'. So not only is it wrong to associate drains or any kind of open drainage like gutters with 'Water Dragons' since Water Dragons are supposed to be natural bodies of water, it is wrong to use this approach when you do not have absolutely flat land. Finally, it is wrong to imagine that you can actually 'construct' a Water Dragon since to be a Water Dragon in the first place, it needs to be natural, not man-made.

It is wrong to imagine that you can actually 'construct' a Water Dragon since to be a Water Dragon in the first place, it needs to be natural, not man-made.

No classical Feng Shui text mentions drains or visible drainage systems in lieu of real water. You are constructing a drain and that is exactly what it is. There is no magic or potent Feng Shui to it. If you are lucky, your drain will just remain a drain. If you are not so fortunate, then this drain, far from making you rich, will end up causing problems.

Drains or any form of exposed water channel are a form of Sha Qi known as Merciless Water (more on this in Chapter 3). This is because the water invariably flows in a straight and fast gushing manner, which is not the way we want water to move. Fast moving water is regarded as cutting into the property. If it happens to be positioned very close to the side of the house, it is called Cutting Water. If it flows in front of the Main Door, this is called Cutting Feet Water . Neither formation is favourable in any way.

If you are lucky, your drain will just remain a drain. If you are not so fortunate, then this drain, far from making you rich, will end up causing problems.

Water Myth #3:
There's no such thing as Water Dragon Formulas.

Water Dragon Formulas is the term created by English language books on Water Feng Shui. It is an all-encompassing, romanticised phrase used to describe what classical Feng Shui practitioners plainly refer to as Water Formulas.

Now, the tricky thing about Water Dragon Formulas is that they're not entirely made up. Most of the time, the Water Dragon Formulas you find in English language books on Water Feng Shui are a collection of Water Formulas from several sources such as *Di Li Wu Jue* 地理五訣 *(Earthly Principles Five Verses), Si Ta Shui Ju* 四大水局 *(Four Major Water Structures), Hou Tian Shui Fa* 後天水法 *(Later Heaven Water Method)* and *Fu Xing Shui Fa* 輔星水法 *(Assistant Star Water Method)*. Another favourite source of Water Formulas is a book by late Ming/Early Qing Dynasty Feng Shui master Jiang Da Hong, called *Water Dragon Classics* 水龍經.

Unfortunately, the understanding of how these formulas should be applied is what is wrong.

A number of English language books on Water Feng Shui take the view that drains or drainage systems constructed so the direction of water entry and exit is in accordance with a formula determined by the Facing Direction of the house, will create millionaires and billionaires. The practitioners behind these Water Feng Shui books espouse the view that Water Formulas mentioned in the ancient classics refer to water drainage points. Thus, taking that viewpoint to the next level, artificially constructed waterways or channels ('drains' by any other name) which enter and exit at the directions specified by the formula, will satisfy the requirements of the formula.

This is the wrong interpretation for several reasons. Firstly, the implementation of Water Formulas through the construction of drains or visible drainage systems violates several classical Feng Shui principles, specifically those related to Forms. No classical Feng Shui text will ever espouse the deliberate creation of Sha Qi (which drains will create) in order to achieve prosperity. That's just silly.

Secondly and more importantly, the assumption that the classical texts on Water Formulas were referring to drainage entry and exit points is erroneous. Classical texts like as *Di Li Wu Jue (Earthly Principles Five Verses)*, *Si Ta Shui Ju (Four Major Water Structures)*, *Hou Tian Shui Fa (Later Heaven Water Method)* and *Fu Xing Shui Fa (Assistant Star Water Method)* discuss the flow and movement of **natural waterways** such as rivers. For example, the *Water Dragon Classics*, written by Jiang Da Hong in the late Ming/Early Qing period, is about river formations. The book does not refer or make reference to drainage points, and most certainly did not have drains, ancient or otherwise, in mind when it was written. Indeed, Jiang Da Hong specifically points out that water formations much match the mountains or the Yin components of the environment to have any effect. Therefore if 'water' in the form of man-made waterways or open drainage systems is present but the natural, mountain formation is not, the 'water' is not considered real effective water within the context of Classical Feng Shui.

The Water Dragon Classics, written by Jiang Da Hong in the late Ming/Early Qing period, is about river formations.

So not only is the Water Dragon Formula a myth, but the idea that you can recreate such a non-existent Formula, using drains, is absolutely wrong.

I might add, this whole business of digging ditches and drains around your home is not just an erroneous practice of Feng Shui, it's hideously impractical if you really think about it. For starters, visible drainage or drains are actually mainly only seen in tropical weather countries where there is a large volume of rainwater. You hardly ever see exposed drainage in Europe. In any case, if you happen to live in a country with four seasons, this means that during winter, you will have an ice Water Dragon!

Here's the bottom line on Water Feng Shui which involves constructing drains: it's wrong, it doesn't work and it's ugly. These are all good reasons NOT to implement any kind of Water Feng Shui that involves making drains.

No classical Feng Shui text will ever espouse the deliberate creation of Sha Qi (which drains will create) in order to achieve prosperity.

Water Myth #4:
A Water Dragon Formula can make you a billionaire.

This myth combines several incorrect assumptions. The first incorrect assumption is that Water alone is responsible for creating wealth. This has already been established as false understanding because, as stated in Chapter 1, there are mountain formulas that can also be used for wealth creation.

Secondly, as I have pointed out in Chapter 1, Water's role is to circulate, gather, move and activate the Qi. Water in itself does not generate the Qi. So the whole notion for a Water Formula that can make you rich beyond your dreams is premised on the entirely erroneous assumption that the Water creates the Wealth Qi. When in fact, Water does not create any Qi, nevermind Wealth Qi.

Do not get sucked into the misconception that Water Formulas are all-powerful. All formulas in Feng Shui can be effective if they are used correctly, for the purpose in which they were developed to achieve.

Water Myth #5:
Water Formulas are closely guarded Feng Shui secrets, hence they command a premium.

Water formulas are not closely guarded Feng Shui secrets. They are available for all and sundry at your nearest Chinese book store. Now you might argue, since they are in the Chinese language, they are a secret only to those who can read English. Well, most of these formulas are now  freely available in many reasonably priced English language books on Water Feng Shui. So really, there's no need to break the bank for a formula. And you should be especially skeptical if it comes with the added sales pitch of being 'passed down from teacher to student'.

Water Myth #6:
The falsehood of the Formula.

Often, people are fixated on the idea that if they have the right Water Formula for their home, great wealth is a shoo-in. The fact is that a formula is not the be-all-and-end-all of Feng Shui. It is in fact worth nothing, if you don't know how to apply it, and most importantly, if you don't have the External Formations that are needed to support the formula.

A Feng Shui formula is just a bunch of directions. Just like a cake recipe is just a list of ingredients. Unless you know how the ingredients work together, have the baking skills, and or have the right equipment to enable you to make the cake, it's worth very little. I would go so far as to say a Feng Shui formula is not worth the paper it's printed on because if you have no idea how to use it, or what it actually means, it's as good as worthless.

Myth #7 :
Roving Eyes and Right Side Water.

This theory about water on the right side of the home leading to a roving eye or affairs by the man of the house is one of those old wives' tales that just seems to refuse to go away. I've lost count of the number of anxious clients who have inquired about this matter.

The only time Water can cause a problem with marital relationships or straying is if it happens to activate a Peach Blossom star in the property. But this Peach Blossom Star could be located ANYWHERE and not necessarily the right hand side of the property or Main Door.

Let me dispel this myth once and for all: it's totally false. I would go so far as to say its what I call Feng Shui Science Fiction and absolutely 100 percent made up. There is no mention of such a principle in the classical texts on Feng Shui.

Myth #8 – It's all about The Fish.

As this is a book on aquariums and Feng Shui, I obviously have to address this myth. Many people assume that the number of fish, number of gold to black fish, or the type of fish in an aquarium is intimately connected to the Feng Shui quotient of the property.

Frankly, the fish have been getting a little too much kudos and credit for something which they have absolutely no effect on – the Feng Shui of a property.

There's actually no real need to have fish in the aquarium. You could just place a pump in the aquarium and leave it to circulate the Water and keep it active. The fish simply add an aesthetic quality to the aquarium, and make it less obvious that you're using Feng Shui! So if you want to have fish in the tank, go ahead. But there is no need for any special type of fish, nor do certain types of fish bring more 'luck' than others. Any fish will do.

Water Myth #9:
Any water will do, even if it's a picture of water.

No person would accept the notion that a photo or image of something is the real thing (you can't eat a picture of food now can you?). But when it comes to Feng Shui, anything goes!

When we talk about using Water in classical Feng Shui, we mean real water.

H2O.

The image of water, thoughts of water, and the sound of water are not considered Water in classical Feng Shui. So when a Feng Shui book tells you that you can use an image or picture of water in lieu of real water, think about whether or not you can eat that picture of a bowl of noodles in the menu at the Chinese restaurant in lieu of a 'real' bowl of noodles.

When we talk about using Water in classical Feng Shui, we mean real water.

Spotting the Water Myth

There are many myths, misconceptions and wrong ideas circulating out there about Water and Feng Shui. It is quite frankly impossible to address all of them – indeed, in this section, I have tried to address the more popular ones, as well as those which I have frequently encountered in the course of teaching and consulting. But like Hydra, the minute you think you've dealt with one of these myths, another pops up to replace it!

For those that I have not managed to address, the next chapter explores some of the principles and theories about Water. It will invariably sometimes be difficult to separate the wheat from the chaff, especially since a lot of New Age Feng Shui these days is not always totally made-up and arguably does have some roots or is extrapolated from some principles of classical Feng Shui. But I believe the information afforded to you in the next Chapter will be helpful in giving you the basics about Water and its use in classical Feng Shui. In turn, it may well help you ask the right questions, when you are confronted with the question of whether or not something is a Water Feng Shui Myth.

It will invariably sometimes be difficult to separate the wheat from the chaff, especially since a lot of New Age Feng Shui these days is not always totally made-up and arguably does have some roots or is extrapolated from some principles of classical Feng Shui.

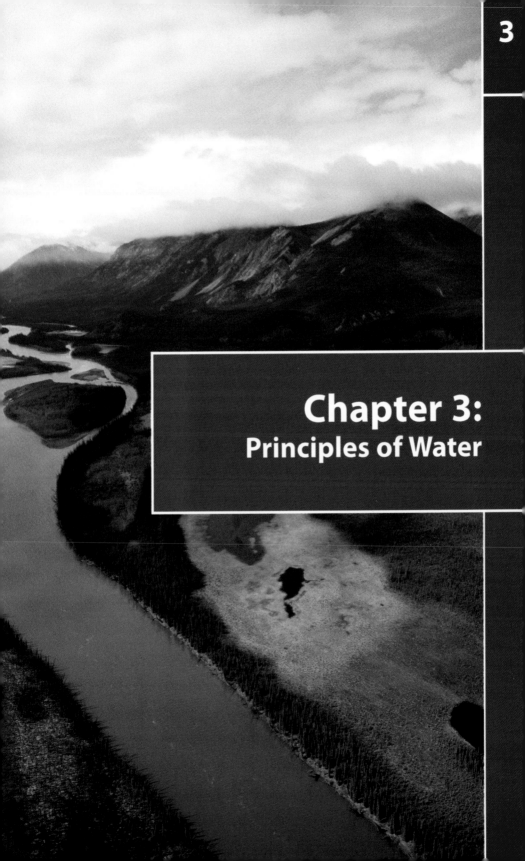

Chapter 3:
Principles of Water

Principles of Water

In this chapter, I want to provide you with some basic principles that relate to the subject of Water and Feng Shui. Now, this is a vast subject – entire classical Feng Shui texts are written on a singular aspect of using Water within a specific landform context, or for a specific purpose. So it is not possible to comprehensively cover everything on the subject of Water and Feng Shui.

In addition, a greater appreciation of how Water is wielded requires a certain level of knowledge about many of the key tenets of Feng Shui such as the Ba Gua, the Hexagrams and Flying Stars. These are discussed in some of my other books on classical Feng Shui and will not be discussed here. So the extent in which I will discuss this subject will naturally be somewhat restricted.

Nonetheless, I am confident that you will find a great deal of the information here helpful towards enabling you to better understand how Water and Feng Shui work, and to avoid the pitfalls and dangers that come with the wrong use of Water for Feng Shui. You will also find you are better able to separate fact from Feng Shui Fiction when it comes to this business of Water Feng Shui and Water Dragons and when you are offered a one in a lifetime billionaire creating Water Formula, for the right price of course!

Water, the Double Edged Sword

Water is what keeps our planet and humans alive. Yet it is also capable of great destruction. A gentle shower is cooling and invigorating but if you've ever stood in the middle of a raging thunderstorm, you'll know rain can also pelt down hard, to the point of being almost painful.

Sentimental Water

In Feng Shui, Water also embodies a dual quality about it. When water is slow and meandering, this type of Water is termed 'sentimental' - this is the kind of Water we like in Feng Shui. When Water flows swiftly, gushing, frothing and thundering, it is merciless and not the kind of Water we like in Feng Shui. Water can reflect Qi, barricade Qi for collection, re-direct Qi, but this applies to both Sheng Qi and Sha Qi! It can be used to soften the impact and blow of Sha Qi, but similarly it can magnify the effects of Sha Qi. It can trap Sha Qi, but also equally trap Sheng Qi.

Merciless Water

True Water is Natural Water

Natural formations of Water such as lakes, creeks and rivers are always prized over man-made water creations like fountains, fishponds and swimming pools. This is because normally, man-made water creations cannot match the scale of naturally occurring Water Formations. You can make a swimming pool, but can you dig a real lake? Not unless you are Emperor Qian Long perhaps.

Naturally occurring Water Formations also have a different advantage over man-made Water Formations.

Natural Water

Man-made Water

Admittedly, water is water, and whether it is natural or man-made, it is still H2O. But natural Water Formations are always a product of their environment – the Water collects and pools where it does, because that is where it is meant to be located. Mountain Formations in the area will almost always conform and match the Water Formations of the area.

The movement and flow of the Qi in this area will be at its most natural, and therefore, most powerful, plentiful and effective. The Qi invariably gathers in a location which renders it easily accessible for collection. In a natural environment, all you have to do is tap into the Qi. You don't need to do any extra legwork.

Man-made environments by contrast almost always involve forcing the Qi to behave in certain ways. For example, if you manufacture a man-made lake or creek, you need to work a lot harder to get it to transport the Qi to the right areas because the mountains in the area may not naturally do this for you. You also need to work harder at directing the Qi to the right places. All this trouble comes from trying to manufacture a specific environment. People also forget that whilst you can man-make the water, it is certainly almost impossible to man-make the mountain.

The two go hand in hand. Mountains are the Yin, Water is the Yang. If you have the Yang without the Yin, then the perfection that is required stemming from Yin and Yang is missing. So making the Water is only one half of the equation – unless you have the Mountain to go with it, there's no Qi to circulate anyway. So the Water really serves no purpose.

Mountains are the Yin

In addition, man-made Water is considered to have finite potential or hold finite capacity as it may dry up, or be moved, or covered. By contrast, natural Water rarely dries up and is regarded to have infinite potential and capacity.

Water is the Yang

Therefore ultimately, natural water is always vastly superior in terms of its efficacy in Feng Shui, compared to man-made water.

Knowing your External from your Internal

External Water refers to Water that is outside of your property (such as in the lawn or patio or open space) or not enclosed within the 4 walls of your home. Internal Water refers to water that is inside your property and enclosed within the 4 walls of your home. Between External Water and Internal Water, External Water is arguably more important, but both types of Water play a part in the Feng Shui of a property.

To appreciate the difference between these two types of Water and how they are used differently, we must understand how Qi moves.

Qi does not just sweep into a property – that would mean it is moving too fast. Qi is also very Yang energy, so sometimes it can be overwhelming. As a rule, we like the Qi to be slow and meandering, and we want it to have the opportunity to settle a little, before it spreads and meanders through the property.

 As such, in Feng Shui, we like to attract the Qi, and allow it to settle and gather, before pulling it into a property. External Water does this very well – a small pond or a receptacle of water outside your home (think 1 gallon tank) will help to attract the Qi in the environment and enable it to settle down and calm down, before you pull it into your property.

By contrast, Internal Water rarely plays the part of collecting and gathering Qi. It is usually used to just activate Qi that is already in the house. Thus, without the External Water to help pull in the Qi from the environment, the Internal Water has no opportunity to play its part. Hence, External Water is much more important than Internal Water in many respects.

Many times however, Feng Shui practitioners may end up simply affording an Internal Water solution because this is a solution that generally is the easiest to implement. In most homes, you can easily find a space for an aquarium and it is an affordable feature, unlike making a fishpond in your front yard. It is also a flexible solution, as it works for apartments, condominiums and homes with tight or no external space such as link-houses.

Location vs Timeliness:
You can't borrow your friend's Water

Ideal water locations fluctuate and change, as the location of the Qi moves through the different Periods 1-9. In each Period, there is a premium location for Water, and of course, a location where Water should NOT be located. As such, when a Feng Shui practitioner evaluates a Water Formation, be it man-made or natural, Internal or External, foremost on their minds is whether or not it is timely. Meaning, it is in the right location given the prevailing cycle of the Qi.

As such, it cannot be assumed that what is good Water location for one property, is necessarily the same for another property, even when they have the same Facing Direction. The Water may be timely for one property, but not timely for another. As such, it is not wise to be fixed on the issue of the location of Water alone – we must also consider if its location is appropriate, given the prevailing cycle of Qi of the Period.

Water within your compound and Water beyond your compound

When we talk about where Water is located, we do not confine ourselves in Feng Shui to merely a geographical or directional context. We also examine the location of the Water in the context of whether it is within the boundaries of the property (or within your compound) or beyond the boundaries of your property (or outside your compound).

The difference of water within a compound and beyond a compound is subtle but significant. We regard water within the compound or property boundary as your water. Water beyond your compound or outside your property boundary is other people's water (or public water if you like, if it does not reside in someone's compound).

In both instances, the Water is usable by you. But the outcome and manner of use of the Water is different, depending on whether it is within your compound or outside your compound. When the Water is within your compound, it refers to opportunities for growth (financial or otherwise) which stem from your own efforts, or your own coffers. This means, you do it the hard way and don't leverage off other people.

By contrast, water that is beyond your boundaries is regarded as opportunities for growth or wealth advancement that involve leveraging of other people. Examples of this include staring a business with capital investment from family members rather than your own money, or say, co-investing in a business with other people.

Ideally, we want the water to be in the right location for the cycle of Qi of that Period, outside the compound, but clearly visible from the property, specifically the Main Door. Thus, we kill two birds with one stone of having both External Water, and water which enables us to leverage opportunities. And five gold stars if this water happens to be natural as this means the opportunities and potential that will flow to your property are infinite.

Distinguishing Sha Qi and Sheng Qi Water

As I said at the start of this chapter, Water has a chameleonic quality and it is never possible to say, without qualification, that water is good or bad, generating Sha Qi or Sheng Qi

It depends on the water. And you need to see it, hear it, and observe how it moves, curves and bends, to really know the quality of the Water and whether it is Sha Qi or Sheng Qi. But here are some simple ways that the average person can distinguish between Sha Qi water and Sheng Qi water.

Sha Qi Water Characteristics	Sheng Qi Water Characteristics
Fast moving	Slow moving
Straight and narrow shape	Meandering and wide shape
Restless	Gentle
Loud	Quiet
Smelly and stagnant	Clean and free flowing

It does not matter if the Water conforms to a formula – if it is Sha Qi Water, then the sector or area where the Sha Qi strikes will be negatively affected. Furthermore, in Feng Shui, the rule is that Forms over-rule Formulas. Negative forms will, in effect, render the formula unusable or significantly less efficacious.

However, Feng Shui also takes the view that whilst it is not always possible to have Sheng Qi water, you should try not to have Sha Qi Water.

The Yin and Yang of Water

At the heart of Feng Shui is the core idea of Yin and Yang in perfect balance. Mountains, which are Yin, are such because they are immovable. Water, which is Yang, is such because it is active and always moving.

Yet if we examine the concept of Yin and Yang closer, we will find that the harmony is achieved by ensuring we have both Yin and Yang, but also, Yin within the Yang, and Yang within the Yin.

In other words, we do not want that which is Yang to be Pure Yang, and that which is Yin to be Pure Yin. That which is Pure Yin is without life. That which is Pure Yang is without growth. Think of it as life where there is no progress, only stagnation, or life where there is constant movement, but no opportunity to stop and smell the roses. Neither is desirable. And neither is the true definition of Yin and Yang.

Thus, the concept of 'Yin within the Yang, Yang within the Yin' captures the true meaning of yin and yang, balance, harmony and perfection within the world of Metaphysics.

Thus, in Mountains, which we classify broadly as Yin, we can have Yang Mountains based on their shape or form. Similarly, in Water, which we classify broadly as Yang, we can have Yin Water or Yang, based on its shape or form. And as such, we cannot say that if something is Yin, it is negative and something is Yang, it is always positive.

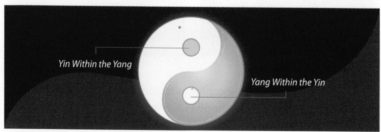

Yin within the Yang, Yang within the Yin.

It is wrong to say that if Water has Yin qualities, it is bad, whilst if Water has Yang qualities it is good. The only time you can arguably be decisive on Water as 'good' or 'bad' is if you are confronted with a case of Sha Qi water and Sheng Qi Water.

In fact, we want Water to have some Yin attributes in it, as a means of achieving that coveted Yin within the Yang, Yang within the Yin balance and perfection. How do we achieve this?

The polarity of Water (meaning whether it is Yin Water or Yang Water) is defined by its state and appearance. Water in itself is already Yang. So when it meanders, flows gently and quietly, it is already manifesting Yin qualities, and thus is regarded as Yin Water. Water can be clean or murky, but as long as it is fast moving, it is still classified as Yang Water.

When Water is classified as Yang Water it is regarded as too active and too strong. It does not enable Qi to gather or collect or accumulate. In general, it is the preferred form for Water.

Water Forms

It is quite impossible for me to discuss the subject of Water Forms here exhaustively. The subject itself is covered in several of the classics like *Shui Long Jing* 水龍經 *(Water Dragon Classics)*, *Xue Xin Fu* 雪心輔 *(Snow Heart Classics)* and *Ru Di Yan* 入地眼 *(Entering Earth Eye)* and the only way to actually comprehensively understand the subject is to read all the classics. However, in introducing the topic here, my aim is to enable you to gain some appreciation of the concept of Water Forms.

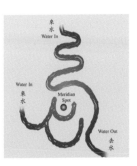

The study of Water Forms, like the study of Mountain Forms, involves looking at the shape of the river, and the way the water flows, the estuaries and deltas, and then determining its star form. The star forms can relate to an element (ie: a Wood Star river) or one of the stars in the 28 Constellations (ie: a Greedy Wolf River). There are 9 basic river forms, and a further 9 incarnations of each individual basic river forms. So that's 81 types of formations, for just rivers or moving water. Pools of water such as lakes and ponds also have individual forms, each with a different significance and Feng Shui effect.

For the layperson, this is quite difficult to do because it is quite difficult to see the flow of the water and the curves of the river, unless you have a map. And even with a map, it's not easy to figure out what you are looking at because these days, the shape and bend of a river can be affected by man-made changes to the environment.

The point to appreciate here is that no two rivers are ever exactly the same, and not all natural water is created equal. Some Water Forms, like Heavenly Pool Water Formations, are quite unique and rare, and are only seen in very specific contexts. Others are a little bit more common, like say a Greedy Wolf River (a river that flows in a straight line) and a Huge Door River (a square-like river form). And thus, when we are looking at the use of Water in Feng Shui, where the water is located is but one consideration. The shape of the Water, its form and the type of star it represents, adds a further layer of complexity to the way that particular body of Water can be utilised.

Behind me is a Heavenly Pool Water Formation in Na Mu Cuo Mountain in Tibet.

The Ways of Water

Here's a brief summary of what are some of the principles that Feng Shui practitioners have foremost when evaluating or examining Water in regard to a property:

- Where is the Water? Is it in a timely location for the Period based on the Formulas? Is it within the property or beyond the compound?

- What kind of Water is it? Is it natural or man-made? Is it External or Internal?

- What characteristics and quality does the Water have? Is it sentimental or merciless? Does it bring Sha Qi or Sheng Qi?

- What kind of Water is it? What is its shape? It's form? What stars does it represent?

These are not questions that the layperson will be expected to take into consideration when they are engaged in DIY Feng Shui. If you want to DIY Feng Shui and use Water, Chapter 4 shows you how to do that without too much fuss, and in a completely safe manner. But these are relevant questions that a professional Feng Shui consultant should be taking into consideration when evaluating the Water component of your property's Feng Shui. And these are considerations which any formula, Water Dragon Formula or just plain Water Formula, should reflect if it is an authentic and proper Formula.

3

Chapter 4:
How to use this Book

How to use this Book

Whilst this book has primarily been written for those who wish to make use of Feng Shui in their homes without too much fuss, prospective homeowners may also find this book useful. Certain properties in certain Periods are not conducive to the use of Water to activate the Qi, and thus there is no suitable location for an aquarium in such homes. As the alternative methods that are used to activate the Qi are not as convenient or easy as placing an aquarium, there is a basis to argue that you should avoid purchasing or renting such a property.

As such, this book may also be helpful for those trying to identify a suitable property for purchase or rental, and getting a quick snapshot of whether or not the property can be 'Feng Shui'ed' without too much hassle or effort. If you can't even do something simple like activate the Qi using an aquarium, chances are you going to need a lot more work or renovation to improve the Feng Shui of the property.

Your Aquarium – HERE

In order to ascertain the most favourable location for an aquarium in your home, you will first need to do a small amount of homework. A mere three steps are required so that you can find the right place for an aquarium in your home. They are:

- Ascertaining the Facing Direction of your home
- Demarcating the interior of your home according to the 8 Directions (North, South, East, West, Northeast, Northwest, Southeast, Southwest) – this is applicable to both landed properties and apartments
- Identifying your property's Flying Star chart to determine the most suitable location for an aquarium in your home

In this section, I will show you how to do all of the above (you'll see it's actually really easy). And then after that it's simply a matter of finding an aquarium you like, and putting it in the place it needs to be.

Ascertaining the Facing Direction of your home

If you have read some of my other books like *Feng Shui for Homebuyers*, you should be quite familiar with taking a direction. For those who live in apartments, the process is slightly different - you may want to read *Feng Shui for Apartment Buyers* if you find you are having some trouble taking a direction for your apartment building as the subject is expansively dealt with in *Feng Shui for Apartment Buyers*.

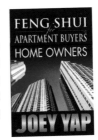

To find out the Facing Direction of your home, be it landed property or an apartment, you will need a compass. You do not need to use a Luo Pan – a scout's compass will do. The best is an automatic compass as it is not confusing and very easy to use.

Step 1: Find the Facing of your Home

The Facing of your home is the direction in which your home has been built to face. The best guide of the direction in which the home has been built to face is to look at the façade. If the façade is not obvious, then ascertain which is the most Yang side of the property. The most Yang side of the property is defined as the property which receives the most light, or which faces a main or busy street or road. That is usually the Facing when the façade is not obvious.

Facing

Do not use the location of the Main Door as an indication of the Facing of your home as there are many instances where the Main Door does not share the Facing of the building.

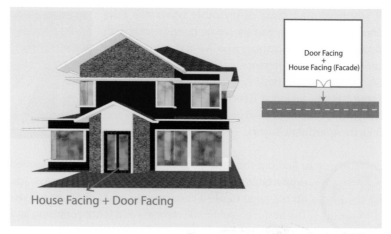

The house facing and the door facing are the same direction.

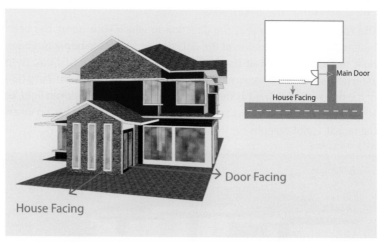

Don't assume that the Main Door always indicates the facing of the house; this illustration shows you an example of when the house facing and door facing are not in the same direction.

Step 2: Stand at the Facing of the property, with your back to the property. Hold up the compass and ascertain the Facing Direction of the property. In Classical Feng Shui, there are 24 possible Facing Directions, as each of the 8 basic directions are trisected into 3 sub-sectors. So a property doesn't just face say, East, it can have a East 1, East 2 or East 3 Facing Direction.

Check the list below to ascertain which is the Facing Direction of your property, based on the degrees of the compass. If you use a Luo Pan or my Mini-Compass, you won't need to refer to this chart.

Gua	Direction	24 Mountains				Degrees
離 Li	South	S1	Bing	丙	Yang Fire	157.6 - 172.5
		S2	Wu	午	Horse (Yang Fire)	172.6 - 187.5
		S3	Ding	丁	Yin Fire	187.6 -202.5
坤 Kun	Southwest	SW1	Wei	未	Goat (Yin Earth)	202.6 - 217.5
		SW2	Kun	坤	South West (Earth)	217.6 - 232.5
		SW3	Shen	申	Monkey (Yang Metal)	232.6 - 247.5
兌 Dui	West	W1	Geng	庚	Yang Metal	247.6 - 262.5
		W2	You	酉	Rooster (Yin Metal)	262.6 - 277.5
		W3	Xin	辛	Yin Metal	277.6 - 292.5
乾 Qian	Northwest	NW1	Xu	戌	Dog (Yang Earth)	292.6 - 307.5
		NW2	Qian	乾	North West (Metal)	307.6 - 322.5
		NW3	Hai	亥	Pig (Yin Water)	322.6 - 337.5
坎 Kan	North	N1	Ren	壬	Yang Water	337.6 - 352.5
		N2	Zi	子	Rat (Yang Water)	352.6 - 7.5
		N3	Gui	癸	Yin Water	7.6 - 22.5
艮 Gen	Northeast	NE1	Chou	丑	Ox (Yin Earth)	22.6 - 37.5
		NE2	Gen	艮	North East (Earth)	37.6 - 52.5
		NE3	Yin	寅	Tiger (Yang Wood)	52.6 - 67.5
震 Zhen	East	E1	Jia	甲	Yang Wood	67.6 - 82.5
		E2	Mao	卯	Rabbit (Yin Wood)	82.6 - 97.5
		E3	Yi	乙	Yin Wood	97.6 - 112.5
巽 Xun	Southeast	SE1	Chen	辰	Dragon (Yang Earth)	112.6 - 127.5
		SE2	Xun	巽	South East (Wood)	127.6 -142.5
		SE3	Si	巳	Snake (Yin Fire)	142.6 - 157.5

Demarcating the Interior of your Home

The purpose of demarcating the interior of your home is to enable you to determine which rooms or areas of your home fall within which one of the 8 directions. To do this you will need:

- Floor plan of your home (preferably an architect or draftsman's version)

- Red pen and a ruler

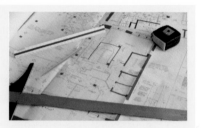

The interior of a property is always demarcated using the nine grids method. Here is how you do it:

Step 1: Super-impose the Nine Grids over your property floor plan.

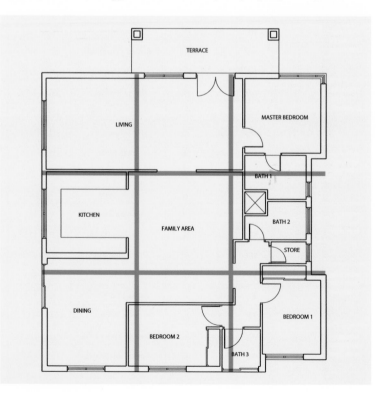

Step 2: Mark the Facing Direction in the center square of the grid where the front of your home is located. For example, if your home faces East (either East 1, 2, or 3), mark East in the center square of the three squares that correspond with the front of your property.

Step 3: Mark out the rest of the directions in an orderly, clock-wise fashion.

You should now be able to determine which section or area or room in your home, corresponds with each of the 8 Directions.

Identifying the Flying Star Chart of your property

Based on the Facing Direction of your property, find the relevant Flying Star chart in the pages overleaf.

For ease of reference, the charts are divided up into Period 7 properties and Period 8 properties. How do you know which period is applicable to your property?

If you moved into your home between **1984 - 2003**, then your property is a Period 7 property. All the charts relevant to Period 7 properties are located at page 47.

If you moved into your home between **2004 – 2023**, then your property is a Period 8 property. All the charts relevant to Period 8 properties are located at page 81.

Apartments and Move-In Dates

The move-in date is only used to determine the chart of the property when it is landed property being considered. In the case of apartments, the date that you moved into the apartment is not the correct reference. Instead, you should use the date in which the apartment building was first occupied.

If you are living in a relatively new apartment building (completed say, after 2004) and you are one of the early occupants or original owners, then use the date you moved in. If you are living in an apartment building that was completed between 1984 - 2003, but you only moved into the building in 2005, DO NOT use the date you moved in. Your property would be considered a Period 7 building, so use the charts relevant to Period 7, not Period 8.

If you are living in an old apartment that was built and occupied before 1984, then the charts here will not be applicable to your property, irrespective of your move-in date. As such, you may need to seek the advice of a qualified Feng Shui consultant to determine the appropriate location for an aquarium in your property.

Once you have the right Flying Star chart for your property, you will find a simple chart that tells you the most suitable locations for an aquarium. There is also a Commentary section, for those of you who are interested in some of the technical explanations behind the choice of locations and some additional extras for those who want to learn more.

E		SE		S
	2 9	1 8	5 3	
	6	**7**	**3**	
NE	6 4	9 7	3 1	SW
	2	**8**	**5**	
	4 2	8 6	7 5	
	4	**9**	**1**	
N		NW		W

Facing SE2 / SE3

Where do you put your aquarium?

Best Location	Southeast
2nd Best Location	Southwest
3rd Best Location	East

If you are looking for a fuss-free approach, just place the aquarium in the location that is most convenient for you, based on the choice of locations afforded. If you are inclined to do a little more work, you may want to see if you can place the aquarium in a part of your home that also has a positive effect on your career, or which has a connecting effect on your business or your profession.

In some properties, there are up to three locations you can use, so if one location is not suitable (for example, it's a closet, or the kitchen), then opt for the secondary location. You will also find that certain properties are NOT suited to the use of water in any part of the home. In such instances, I have indicated some of the possible solutions in the Commentary section.

The Commentary section also includes some references to where Water should not be located, and also, to some broader formulas which involve incoming roads or water. These are quite technical in nature and can be confusing or even alarming to the layperson. My advice is not to be alarmed or fearful if you find you are confused by some of the Commentaries. Instead, focus on what you can do (locate your aquarium in the right place) and if you can, make sure that there is no water (in the form of a pond, lake, large body of water or aquarium) where I have stipulated there should not be any water.

Why Aquariums?

You might be wondering – why have I prescribed an aquarium rather than say, suggesting a water feature, or some other water-storage receptacle? Why the aquarium?

Aquariums have been the preferred choice of Feng Shui consultants when it comes to using Water for many reasons. Here are a few of them:

- Aquariums are aesthetically pleasing – they look nice, and many people get pleasure or feel a calming effect from watching fish swim.

- Aquariums do not attract suspicion – although it is a bit of an open secret that the presence of an aquarium is a sign of 'Feng Shui At Work', it could also indicate otherwise. In general, people are less likely to look twice (or think you superstitious or a Feng Shui fanatic) if they saw an aquarium in your home, compared to say if they walked into your home and saw a gigantic water feature with 8 levels and a money toad in the center.

- Aquariums are easy to maintain and keep clean – especially in this day and age wherein you can hire someone to come and keep it clean.

- Aquariums are transparent and usually open at the top – this fulfils the need for the Water to be both seen and exposed.

- Aquariums enable the Water to be kept active – by placing fish, or simply placing a water pump in the tank, you can keep the Water active, which is important in maintaining the movement of the Qi in the area.

- Aquariums are easy – water features pose aesthetic issues, an indoor pool poses renovation issues, crying walls are expensive to maintain, and swimming pools not an option for everyone. Aquariums can be used in homes, offices, apartments, condominiums – practically anywhere and everywhere.

A word on the Water Formulas Chosen for this Book

A limited number of Formulas has been used in the writing of this book and in the prescription of certain locations for aquariums. I want to emphasis LIMITED because Water Formulas are manifold in the study of Feng Shui. Water Formulas also vary in level of complexity. So by no means is this book an exhaustive approach to the locating of Water in the form of an aquarium.

I have mainly based the locations selected for aquariums on the San Yuan Water Formulas, which encompass Xuan Kong Flying Stars and Dragon-Gate Eight Formations. I chose the San Yuan approach to Water because its effects are generally quicker, it works generally without the need for analyzing External Landforms and it doesn't require you to dig drains or try to recreate the Yang Tze River in your backyard. In other words, it's easy to implement and effective in its outcome.

Yet equally, you will find this book does not utilise simplistic or generic techniques. This book does not endorse or practice the common prescription of placing Water at the Facing Stars #8, #9 and #1 because these are the Wealth Stars for Period 8. That would be overly simplistic, highly generic and worse, an approach that ignores all the other, and more important principles in play that extend beyond Flying Stars (which honestly, is only a small system in the grand scheme of Feng Shui systems).

It is for this reason that you will find that I do not always recommend activating the Facing #8, #9 or #1 in every instance. There are some instances where I expressly tell you NOT to use Water in these locations as this violates the Direct Spirit of Period 8, or violates San Yuan Xuan Kong principles on Water Placement. In some instances, you will also find I expressly forbid the use of Water in entirety as these properties are not conducive to the use of or placement of Water.

The Limitations of this Book

Whilst using water according to the techniques outlined here will bring positive results, but they will be *limited results*.

Internal Feng Shui, which is what is mainly what this book focuses on, is inherently limited in its outcome. This is because the greater external environment is always the final arbitrator of the quality of the Feng Shui affecting a property. Internal Feng Shui can help improve matters, but within a limited scope only. You can't make a silk purse out of a sow's ear, so goes the saying.

Internal Feng Shui can help improve matters, but within a limited scope only. You can't make a silk purse out of a sow's ear, so goes the saying.

Furthermore, because the focus here is keeping things simple and quick, only San Yuan Flying Stars techniques and Water Formulas have been used. Within the grand scale of classical Feng Shui, this is but one technique that a consultant may use, amongst others like Xuan Kong Da Gua. San Yuan Flying Stars is also not the most effective or powerful Feng Shui system out there, so this also works to limit the results. However, I want to emphasise that this also means the techniques you are using will be very safe. As a consultant and practitioner, I am very mindful of the need to go with the principle of safety first. Powerful techniques invariably require better technical skills, immaculate judgment and of course, sound technical knowledge to solve the problems at hand. This is why beginners or laypersons are not encouraged to implement these techniques in the first place. It must not just be easy, but it must also be safe.

To keep things simple, I have also limited the charts to Period 7 and Period 8 homes as in my experience, these are the majority of the properties that are out there. This does mean that if your house is a Period 6 or pre-Period 6 property, the content of this book will not be applicable to you. You may therefore wish to seek the assistance of a Feng Shui consultant if you wish to utilise Feng Shui in your home or property.

The operative limitation of this book is 'realistic expectations.' It is fine to expect modest improvement, but do not expect drastic change or extreme change to your fortunes. I must also add that you should not expect Feng Shui to work magic. It is not magic. You still have to work hard, make the effort and push yourself. Preferably you also need to make sure that you are not straying too far from your Destiny Code, as defined by your BaZi.

But I maintain that doing something is always better than doing nothing. And since Feng Shui accounts for 33% of the equation (the other being Man Luck and Heaven Luck), attempting to make use of Feng Shui is better than not trying at all.

Your Aquarium Here   **45**

Chapter 5:
HOMES FACING IN PERIOD 7

South 1 (丙) Facing Homes in Period 7

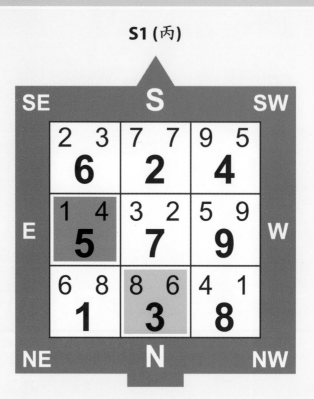

S1 (丙)

SE	S	SW
2 3 **6**	7 7 **2**	9 5 **4**
E		W
1 4 **5**	3 2 **7**	5 9 **9**
6 8 **1**	8 6 **3**	4 1 **8**
NE	N	NW

Where do you put your aquarium?

Best Location	East
2nd Best Location	North

Commentary

Locating an aquarium in the East of a South 1 Period 7 home is most favourable for those working in the public relations, marketing or sales fields, or who own businesses involved in or related to public relations, marketing or sales. It is also particularly good for households with school-going children as the Qi is also favourable for scholastic and academic pursuits. If there also happens to be real water flowing in from the East direction or a road entering at the East direction, this is an even better formation, known as "Early Heaven Water". This type of formation generates wealth through powerful connections, strong networking or by virtue of status or position.

If you locate your aquarium in the North of a South 1 Period 7 house, you need to make sure that the Northwest and North sectors of the property are connected or are easily accessible (such as being connected by a door, or constitute one large room). It is only in such an instance that the aquarium located in the North is able to be truly effective and bring about status, power and authority to the occupants. Such a formation is particularly favourable for professionals (doctors, engineers, accountants, lawyers), creating opportunities to land lucrative and highly profitable jobs. For those in the corporate management field, this combination of aquarium in the North and connecting or open space in the North and Northwest is also favourable as it opens up opportunities for high paying jobs.

South 1 Period 7 homes which also have a large open space or open area (known as "Virtual Water") in the Northeast sector of the property will benefit in Period 8 (2004-2023) specifically. This is because the Northeast is a favourable for "Virtual Water." I must emphasise that "Virtual Water" is NOT actual Water. In a South 1 Period 7 home, you DO NOT want to see real water in the Northeast. It must only be "Virtual Water", in the form of a large open space or open area.

Virtual Water in the Northwest sector of a South 1 Period 7 home brings the greatest financial benefit to individuals who are working in a creative field or in an academic industry, such as writers, scholars, educators and those in the creative or education business.

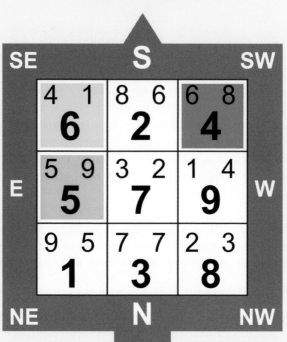

S2 (午) / S3 (丁)

Where do you put your aquarium?

Best Location	Southwest
2nd Best Location	East
3rd Best Location	Southeast

Commentary

Southwest water in the form of an aquarium at this location satisfies the principle of Direct-Indirect Spirit and also activates the Wealth Star of Period 8, which is the #8 Facing Star. In general, this location is a highly favourable location for overall improvement in wealth and progress in career-related matters. This location denotes a steady consistent advancement in wealth through working one's way up the ladder slowly.

Water in the East on the other hand is better for those who are looking to advance their wealth through investments. However, the caveat for East water in a South 2 or South 3 Period 7 home is that having an external body of water (a pond, a lake, or a river in the East sector) is much more beneficial than Internal Water, which is what aquariums and water features are considered. So whilst you can put an aquarium or water feature in the East, the outcome will not be as substantial as compared to a property with a lake or pond in the East sector. The East location for Internal Water is also more beneficial if the occupants are Gua #2, Gua #4 and Gua #9.

Where the primary breadwinner or sole occupant of the household is either an entrepreneur, involved in a start-up business or is a person who earns their income through creative skills and talents, then the Southeast is a better location for an aquarium. This location also generates wealth, but is more conducive to those in the creative fields, or who are starting up a business.

If a South 2 or South 3 Period 7 property also has an incoming road at the East sector, or incoming Water at the East, then the property is said to benefit from "Early Heaven Water." Wealth is acquired through connections with individuals of high status or with powerful positions in society.

Southwest 1 (未) Facing Homes in Period 7

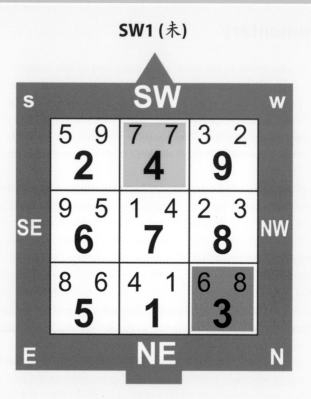

SW1 (未)

Where do you put your aquarium?

Best Location	North
2nd Best Location	Southwest

Commentary

An aquarium in the North is the best location for a Southwest 1 Period 7 property overall. It is positive for both wealth matters and career matters. Where the occupants are involved in the trading, retailing, transport, logistics or Water-element businesses, this aquarium location is particularly favourable. It is also a good aquarium location for occupants who are involved in or working within the Entertainment industry.

Although the Southwest is the secondary location, it would be a better location for the aquarium in a Southwest 1 Period 7 house if the main breadwinner is in the banking or finance industry. This water location is generally more favourable for those involved in the sales, communication, self-improvement, marketing, seminar and education businesses or industries.

If there is an open space, or a road coming in at the East sector, "Later Heaven Water" is considered to be present. This type of water has a significantly positive effect on career progression, resulting in promotions or career advancement that is also favourable for wealth. It is also a good formation for those who make a living from playing sport.

Southwest 1 facing Period 7 properties must not have water, either Internal or External, in the Northwest sector. This is an unfavourable location for water, indicating a loss of wealth as a result of legal problems, disputes or arguments.

Southwest 2 (坤) or Southwest 3 (申) Facing Homes in Period 7

SW2 (坤) / SW3 (申)

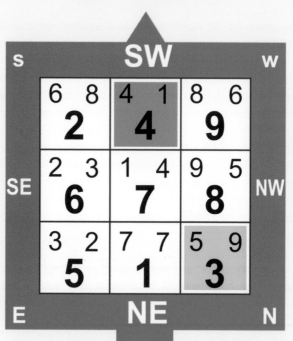

Where do you put your aquarium?

Best Location	Southwest
2nd Best Location	North

Commentary

The Southwest is the most beneficial overall location for Water in the Southwest 2 or Southwest 3 Period 7 property. An aquarium in the Southwest is favourable for wealth and also beneficial for career advancement. Wealth improvement is steady rather than sudden, but is more beneficial if the occupants are involved in the scholastic or academic fields (professors, writers, teachers) or those in the creative or artistic and entertainment industries such as singers, musicians, actors and directors.

The North location is more favourable for those seeking to grow their wealth through long-term investments rather than through salaried employment means.

In a Southwest 2 or Southwest 3 Period 7 property, there should not be a road or water exiting at the East sector. This is a negative water formation that denotes a loss of assets and property, and also is risky for married couples as it denotes miscarriage or fertility problems.

West 1 (庚) Facing Homes in Period 7

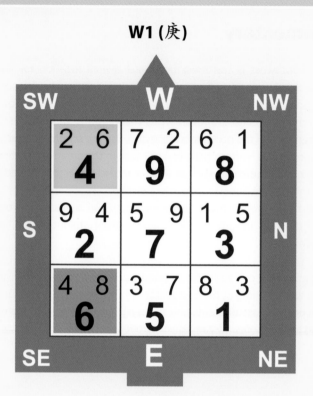

W1 (庚)

Where do you put your aquarium?

Best Location	Southeast
2nd Best Location	Southwest

Commentary

With an aquarium in the Southeast, the fortunes of the occupants will be positive, but also show quick and expansive progress. Entrepreneurs, or those who's jobs involve a measure of entrepreneurial skill, will find that this location helps them be more resourceful or their ability to make better use of available resources enhances their business success.

By contrast, an aquarium in the Southwest would probably be more favourable if a majority of the occupants of the household are in professional fields. This water location brings about the accumulation of wealth through investments in property or tangible assets.

For West 1 Period 7 properties, there should not be a water or road existing at the Northeast direction. This is a formation known as "Water Clashing Through Early Heaven" and creates a risk of loss of wealth as a result of health problems or health challenges.

West 2 (酉) or West 3 (辛) Facing Homes in Period 7

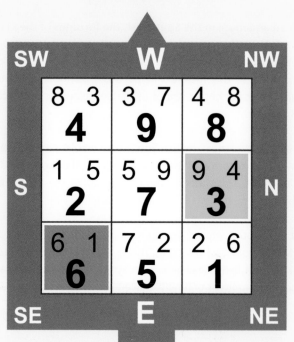

W2 (酉) / W3 (辛)

SW	W	NW
8 3 **4**	3 7 **9**	4 8 **8**
S		N
1 5 **2**	5 9 **7**	9 4 **3**
6 1 **6**	7 2 **5**	2 6 **1**
SE	E	NE

Where do you put your aquarium?

Best Location	Southeast
2nd Best Location	North

Commentary

Water in the Southeast activates Qi that is particularly conducive for those who make their living in the literary or military arts fields. 'Military arts' does refer to those who have chosen to be professional soldiers, but its modern derivative has been expanded to include sports and also those who engage in professional fields that relate to the physique or involve physical activity such as physiotherapists and chiropractors.

If the main breadwinner or a majority of the household occupants are in the public relations, marketing, entertainment or fields which involve networking and building relationships, then locating the aquarium at the North position is better.

Should there be water exiting at the South in the form of a drain, actual water or a road, this is not a favourable formation. It is known as "Water Clashing Through Later Heaven" and indicates a risk of the household occupants losing wealth as a result of fraud, embezzlement, being cheated or through mishaps and accidents.

Northwest 1 (戌) Facing Homes in Period 7

Facing NW1 (戌)

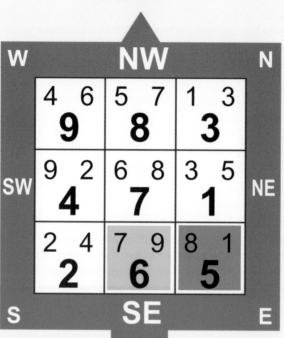

Where do you put your aquarium?

Best Location	East
2nd Best Location	Southeast

Commentary

Locating an aquarium in the East is favourable for business owners, entrepreneurs and professionals. Those in the employ of others will see positive progress as far as promotions go, whilst business owners and entrepreneurs will experience expansion opportunities. Both groups will also find they have help and assistance from mentors and Noble People.

The Southeast is conducive for wealth growth and investment opportunities, but is particularly suited to those in Fire related businesses such as food and beverage, restaurants, beauty, energy and technology-related industries.

If there is also a road or water entering at the Southwest direction, in addition to an aquarium in the Southeast, then the "Receiving Early Heaven Water" formation is regarded as fulfilled. This formation is particularly favourable for females, and denotes success with real-estate opportunities, profitable property investments and an advancement in net worth via the expansion of assets owned.

Northwest 2 (乾) or Northwest 3 (亥) Facing Homes in Period 7

NW2 (乾) / NW3 (亥)

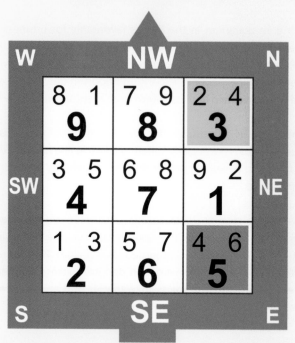

Where do you put your aquarium?

Best Location	East
2nd Best Location	North

Commentary

Water in the East is better if the main bread-winner of the household is involved in a business that is built around a partnership or which requires the use of many partners or joint-ventures in order to succeed. Locating an aquarium in the East is generally favourable for wealth, although it tends to have the effect of producing opportunities for residual income.

North is a good location for Northwest 2 and Northwest 3 Period 8 homes where the occupants are involved in creative, scholastic and academic fields. Entrepreneurs with businesses that involve beauty products, slimming products or the fashion or textiles industry will also benefit from having Water at the North.

For Northwest 2 and Northwest 3 Period 7 homes, there should not be water exiting in the West or a road that exits at the West sector. This is regarded as "Water Clashing through Later Heaven" – this formation, if present, indicates the occupants will have gambling or betting-related financial problems, and results in loss of wealth through mismanagement or ill-advised or unwise decisions related to money matters.

North 1 (壬) Facing Homes in Period 7

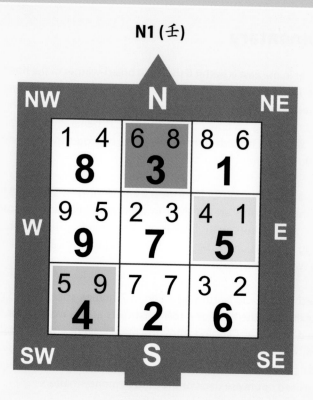

Where do you put your aquarium?

Best Location	North
2nd Best Location	Southwest
3rd Best Location	East

Commentary

Between the three locations, although the North is the best location for the aquarium, this is a more 'generic' location. It has the effect of increasing wealth opportunities across the board and does not particularly favour any one particular profession or industry. So if the household occupants are a mixture of professionals and non-professionals, this is probably the best location to choose.

Water in the Southwest is generally better for those who are looking to generate wealth through investments, specifically property and real estate investments.

Placing an aquarium in the East is best for those who rely on academic, creative or scholastic endeavors to create wealth. So for example, university professors, scientific researchers, academics or graphics designers would benefit more if they placed their aquarium in the East of a North 1 Period 7 property. This location also ensures help from mentors and Noble People, and also indicates positive health.

North 2 (子) or North 3 (癸) Facing Homes in Period 7

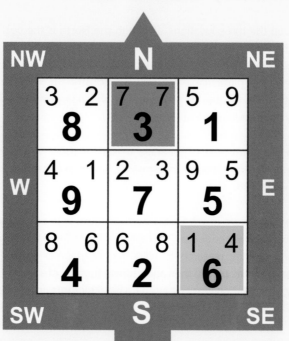

N2 (子) / N3 (癸)

Where do you put your aquarium?

Best Location	North
2nd Best Location	Southeast

Commentary

With an aquarium in the North, the Indirect-Direct Spirit principle is perfectly observed here and this household will have excellent wealth opportunities until the year 2043. It is a particularly favourable water location if the occupants are largely entrepreneurs or business owners, and specifically if their businesses involve the entertainment industry, speaking or motivational/self-help industry, marketing and public relations, as well as general trading.

If the aquarium is placed in the Southeast, this is more favourable for those who need to rely on a good reputation, or a specific reputation associated with their product or service, in order to make money. For example, those in academic, scholastic, fashion or design fields should favour this location, over the North location, for their home aquarium. This position is also good for windfall gains from investments.

For North 2 or North 3 Facing Period 7 properties, any water or road that exits at the East direction is regarded as fulfilling a negative formation known as "Water Clashing Early Heaven." Having water or a road that exits at this direction indicates the occupants run the risk of losing wealth due to sabotage, legal disputes or professional quarrels, and corporate divorce.

5

Northeast 1 (卅) Facing Homes in Period 7

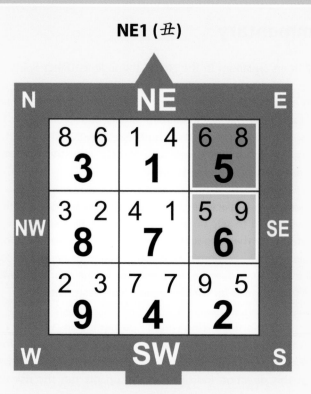

NE1 (卅)

Where do you put your aquarium?

Best Location	**East**
2ⁿᵈ Best Location	**Southeast**

Commentary

An aquarium in the East opens up opportunities for the occupants to expand their wealth and increase their net worth through opportunities that generate multiple streams of income. For example, they may be professionals who have invested in several businesses. Alternatively, it indicates opportunities for entrepreneurs to start a business with multiple sources of revenue.

By contrast, Water in the Southeast denotes obtaining wealth through knowledge or financial savvy and intelligence. Opportunities to create wealth come from smart investing, for example, or through knowledge about wealth management. If in addition to an aquarium in the Southeast, the property also has a road or water incoming at the Southeast, then the "Water Incoming from Later Heaven" formation is fulfilled. This indicates not just wealth, but windfall opportunities that generate tremendous wealth.

Northeast 2 (艮) or Northeast 3 (寅) Facing Homes in Period 7

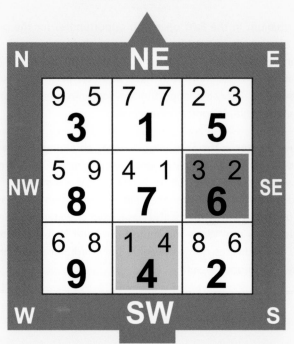

NE2 (艮) / NE3 (寅)

Where do you put your aquarium?

Best Location	Southeast
2ⁿᵈ Best Location	Southwest

Commentary

The Northeast 2 and Northeast 3 Facing Period 7 property is unique in that all the positive Facing Stars #8, #9 and #1 are not located in sectors that allow for Water, per the Direct-Indirect Spirit principle. As such, a different approach has to be utilised, and one has to go beyond mere Flying Stars into advanced Xuan Kong techniques.

The Southeast contains the #3 and #2 stars, but it is the Later Heaven sector. Locating an aquarium here is regarded as "Later Heaven Water," which brings about windfall gains and huge opportunities for wealth generation, specifically through property transactions, sales or investments.

Water in the Southwest is better for those in academic or scholastic fields but is also favourable for those engaged in jobs or businesses that relate to network marketing or property development.

East 1 (甲) Facing Homes in Period 7

E1 (甲)

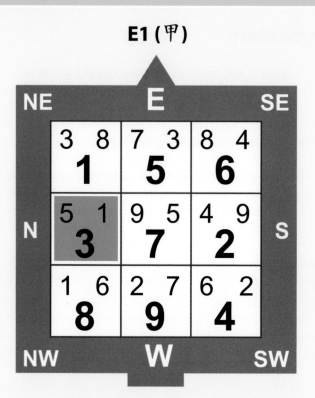

Where do you put your aquarium?

Best Location	North 3

Commentary

Positioning of an aquarium specifically in the North 3 area is favourable for those individuals who are in specialist professional fields (such as doctors who are specialists) or those who are in a unique field of practice for example astrologers, metaphysicians or archeologists. Locating water at the North 3 sector is particularly positive for long-term wealth and asset growth. If there is also incoming Water (in the form of a river, or a road) at the North, combined with an aquarium in the North 3 sector, this is a formation known as "Receiving Later Heaven Water." This formation is particularly favourable for entrepreneurs with a goal of building a business empire.

An alternative formation with water in the North 3 sector is where there is incoming water or an incoming road at the South East direction. This is a formation known as "Receiving Early Heaven Water" – it is favourable for those who rely on connections or networks in order to generate wealth (such as multi-level marketing). This formation also bodes well for the children of the household. They will grow up intelligent, street-wise and highly entrepreneurial and enterprising.

East 2 (卯) or East 3 (乙) Facing Homes in Period 7

E2 (卯) / E3 (乙)

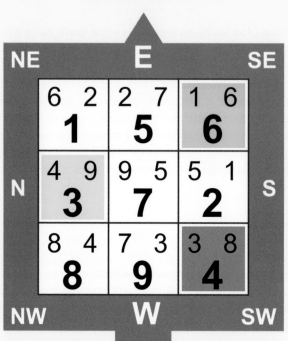

Where do you put your aquarium?

Best Location	Southwest
2ⁿᵈ Best Location	Southeast
3ʳᵈ Best Location	North

Commentary

Locating an aquarium in the Southwest is the most favourable for those working in the property development or building management related industries. Locating water here using an aquarium opens up opportunities in these spheres, but also, opportunities to generate wealth through property transactions or property investment and sales.

If the occupants of the household are mainly professionals, then the Southeast location may be better for an aquarium. This location enables forward and upward career progress for professionals. Known as an "Early Heaven Water" position, activating the Southeast energies with water also means lots of helpful people, mentors and people who assist you on your way up the career ladder.

The North would be a good water location if the occupants of the property rely on popularity and recognition to earn their keep. Thus, those in the public eye such as celebrities, singers, actors or these days, self-help authors and gurus, will find the energies in the North are more conducive to their career needs. Water here brings wealth through the ability to sell yourself as a brand or through product endorsements as you will have popularity and public recognition.

Southeast 1 (辰) Facing Homes in Period 7

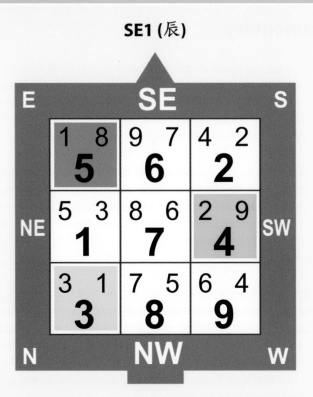

SE1 (辰)

E	SE	S
1 8 **5**	9 7 **6**	4 2 **2**
5 3 **1** NE	8 6 **7**	2 9 **4** SW
3 1 **3** N	7 5 **8**	6 4 **9** W

NW

Where do you put your aquarium?

Best Location	East
2nd Best Location	Southwest
3rd Best Location	North

Commentary

If you live in a Southeast 1 Period 7 property, and you are looking to venture into a business to advance your financial status, then locating the aquarium in the East of the property is ideal. Water in this location is particularly favourable for expanding wealth through the opening up of business opportunities or through the ability to generate business ideas. This water location is particularly conducive to the generation of wealth through an improved business acumen, financial awareness and savvy. This is not to say that this aquarium location is not favourable for those in employment – they will benefit from multiple opportunities for promotions and good support and mentors at work.

Southwest is a good location for an aquarium if your goal is capital gains from assets, or your investment strategy is long-term rather than short-term. For entrepreneurs, this is a good location for an aquarium if your business objective in the medium to long-term future is business expansion. Where the majority of the occupants of the property are female, a Southwest location for the aquarium or water feature should be favoured.

An aquarium in the North is best for households where the main breadwinner is a professional or involved in the sports or physical activity-related fields and industries (such as sports training, professional sportsman, gym owners). It is, however, generally more advantageous for career advancement and progression, or improving status, rather than directly having a positive impact on wealth. This location is particularly favourable for households where the majority of the occupants are male.

Southeast 2 (巽) or Southeast 3 (巳) Facing Homes in Period 7

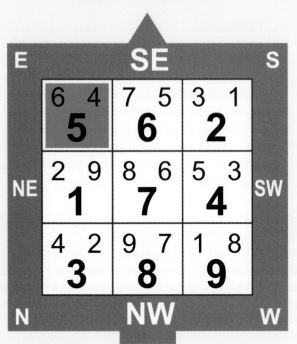

SE2 (巽) / SE3 (巳)

Where do you put your aquarium?

Best Location	East

Commentary

Overall, the Southeast 2 and Southeast 3 Period 7 property is not suited to the use of Internal Water until after the year 2043. The East is the only suitable location for Internal Water placement and even then, it is not a location that is exceptionally effective.

The effects of an aquarium in the East for a Southeast 2 or Southeast 3 Period 7 property is limited particularly to those in artistic, creative or skill-based jobs, or those in the health or alternative health industries.

For this property, there should not be water or a road exiting at the South sector – this is known as "Water Clashing Out Early Heaven." This negative formation denotes a loss of wealth or earning capacity due to health problems, as well as loss of wealth as a result of communication mistakes or problems, or due to negative business relationships.

Water should also not exit at the Northeast sector – this is a negative formation known as "Water Clashing Out Later Heaven." It also brings about a loss of wealth but more as a result of betrayal, backstabbing, sabotage or fraud.

Chapter 6:
HOMES FACING IN PERIOD 8

South 1 (丙) Facing Homes in Period 8

S1 (丙)

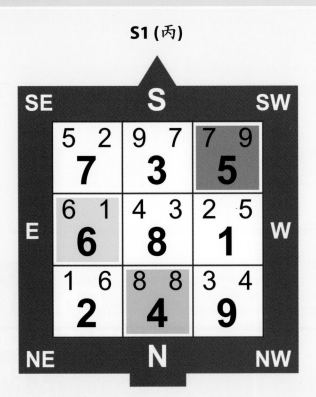

SE	S	SW
5 2 **7**	9 7 **3**	7 9 **5**
6 1 **6**	4 3 **8**	2 5 **1**
1 6 **2**	8 8 **4**	3 4 **9**

E · W · NE · N · NW

Where do you put your aquarium?

Best Location	Southwest
2nd Best Location	North
3rd Best Location	East

Commentary

The Southwest is the best location for an aquarium in a South 1 facing Period 8 property as it generates financial and wealth opportunities for the occupants, and also promotes overall prosperity by way of good health and positive mental attitudes. This water location also brings about fame, popularity and a general improvement in status and reputation. If there is also Water or a Road incoming at the Southwest externally, this Water location is considered supported externally and fulfils the "Receiving Later Heaven Water" formation requirement. When this formation is fulfilled, opportunities for wealth generation or career advancement multiple, and wealth can be derived from multiple revenue streams. Thus, it is much more favourable to occupants who are entrepreneurs or business owners, commission-based income earners or those who are self-employed.

Locating the aquarium at the North is probably the best 'generic' water set-up for a South 1 Period 8 facing property. Locating water at this sector brings about overall wealth luck, and generates steady career opportunities.

An aquarium in the East sector of a South 1 Period 8 property denotes wealth from literary and sporting pursuits, so is favourable for households with occupants who make their money from literary pursuits (writing, teaching) or sporting pursuits. This is also a good location for school-going children as it denotes favourable academic success and also, positive outcomes from sports or extra-curricular activities.

South 2 (午) or South 3 (丁) Facing Homes in Period 8

S2 (午) / S3 (丁)

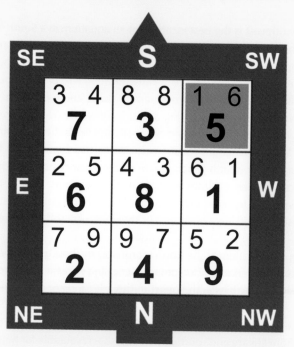

Where do you put your aquarium?

| Best Location | Southwest |

Commentary

South 2 and South 3 Facing Period 8 properties have a limitation in terms of the suitable water placement location and it is restricted to one sector, namely the Southwest. This water location is generally the most beneficial financially and career-wise if the occupants are engaged in jobs or occupations that involve literary endeavours or sports. For example, a writer, graphic designer or a person working in sports marketing will benefit the most from living in a South 2 or South 3 facing Period 8 property, with an aquarium in the Southwest. Of course, if you don't work in any of these industries, you will still benefit from overall positive wealth luck but you will not benefit as much.

If there is also incoming Water or a Road at the Southwest, then the "Receiving Later Heaven Water" formation is considered present. In such an instance, placing an aquarium in the Southwest will activate business and entrepreneurial opportunities for the occupants, and also bring about an overall increase in wealth opportunities.

In a South 2 or South 3 facing Period 8 property, there should not be any Water exiting at the West direction. This means for example, you don't want a drain running out at this direction, or have an infinity pool in this sector. Water exiting at the West sector in a South 2 or South 3 Facing Period 8 property is known as "Water Clashing out Early Heaven" and is a highly negative formation. The impact is primarily on health, and makes the occupants accident-prone. Loss of wealth or income is usually caused by health-related problems or injuries.

Southwest 1 (未) Facing Homes in Period 8

SW1 (未)

	SW	
S		W
7 1 **3**	5 8 **5**	9 3 **1**
3 6 **7**	2 5 **8**	1 4 **9**
SE		NW
4 7 **6**	8 2 **2**	6 9 **4**
E	NE	N

Where do you put your aquarium?

Best Location	Southwest
2nd Best Location	North

Commentary

The Southwest location is a good 'generic' position for Southwest 1 facing Period 8 properties, bringing about a general increase in wealth opportunities, opportunities to increase personal assets and career advancement and promotion. It is also suitable for a property where the occupants are a mixture of business owners, entrepreneurs and those working in the employ of others as it is conducive to wealth generated via business expansion or via promotion and career advancement.

If the aquarium is located in the North, then wealth is derived as a result of help from Noble People or from mentors. Water in this location propels career advancement and results in financial success as a result of strong leadership skills. Thus, this water location is particularly suitable for those in corporate jobs or upper-management positions in large corporations, or those working in public service.

Southwest 2 (坤) or Southwest 3 (申) Facing Homes in Period 8

SW2 (坤) / SW3 (申)

S	SW	W
6 9 **3**	8 2 **5**	4 7 **1**
SE 1 4 **7**	2 5 **8**	3 6 **9** NW
9 3 **6**	5 8 **2**	7 1 **4**
E	NE	N

Where do you put your aquarium?

Best Location	North

Commentary

Locating an aquarium at the North in a Southwest 2 or Southwest 3 facing Period 8 property is particularly advantageous if the occupants or main breadwinner living in the property works or owns a business related to the entertainment, marketing, sales, communication or public relations sectors. Business owners with products or services that have franchising opportunities or openings will also benefit from an aquarium at the North sector if they have a Southwest 2 or Southwest 3 facing Period 8 property.

For the Southwest 2 or Southwest 3 facing Period 8 property, there should not be Water present in the Northwest or exiting at the Northwest. For example, you don't want to have a drain or an infinity pool in the Northwest sector of a Southwest 2 or Southwest 3 facing Period 8 property. Having such a formation will result in the occupants of the household facing career challenges that stem from or result in a loss of authority, power and reputation. As such, this is a particularly damaging formation for properties where the occupants are in public service, politics or corporate management.

West 1 (庚) Facing Homes in Period 8

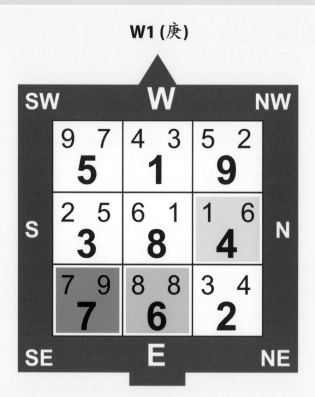

W1 (庚)

Where do you put your aquarium?

Best Location	Southeast
2nd Best Location	East
3rd Best Location	North

Commentary

If using an aquarium in the Southeast, this location brings about a doubling up effect when it comes to wealth and investments. So for example, occupants in employment may find they have an opportunity to leap to a job paying twice their salary, or investment opportunities or assets gain in value two-fold. However, locating an aquarium at this sector is the most beneficial financially for entrepreneurs or business owners engaged in businesses with women or metrosexuals as the primary clientele, such as fashion, accessories, jewellery and the beauty industry.

The East is selected as the secondary location because this location, whilst favourable, has some negative implications on health. Thus, locating an aquarium here will generate short-term wealth opportunities and gains, as well as rapid promotion and advancement for those in employment. But over the long-run, a deterioration of health is part and parcel of using this location for water.

Placing the aquarium in the North does not have any negative implications specifically, but its benefits are quite restricted. In general, unless the breadwinner or the occupants of the household are primarily working or involved in the legal or judicial fields, or in trust or fiduciary-based jobs, the benefits of using this water location are modest at best.

For West 1 facing Period 8 properties, there must not be water present in the South, or water exiting at the South. This formation is known as "Water Clashing Later Heaven" and brings about significant problems and disastrous outcomes as far as wealth loss and career decline are concerned. Water in this position can result in significant financial losses on investments, loss of one's position or even job.

West 2 (酉) or West 3 (辛) Facing Homes in Period 8

W2 (酉) / W3 (辛)

Where do you put your aquarium?

Properties with this Facing cannot utilise internal water in any form.

Commentary

As a rule, West 2 and West 3 facing Period 8 properties are not suited for the placement of internal water. Instead, other alternatives, specifically External Formations and a particular internal-setup, is utilised to activate the Qi.

In such a property, an open space (such as a garden, or balcony or airwell) or a road junction in the Southwest location is the only way to activate the Qi safely and correctly. This has to be accompanied by a bright, spacious room in the Southwest, which opens up to the South, without any walls or doors to obstruct the Qi flow. If this set-up is present, meaning the External and Internal factors are satisfied, then positive outcomes will come about for the occupants if they are involved in construction, property development, plantation, education or consulting industries.

At the same time, there must be no Water located in the Northeast or any water exiting in the Northeast. If this the case, then it becomes a "Water Clashing Out Early Heaven" formation, and will result in a loss of wealth and personal assets, as well as problematic health and tempestuous or difficult personal and professional relationships.

As a general rule, it is unwise to opt for a West 2 or West 3 Facing Home in Period 8 due to these complications. This is especially the case if you are purchasing an apartment or condominium. If for some reason, you find yourself seriously considering purchasing a West 2 or West 3 Facing Period 8 property, I highly recommend getting a Feng Shui consultant to vet the property first to check the External Landforms and features to see if you can satisfy the required set-up.

Northwest 1 (戌) Facing Homes in Period 8

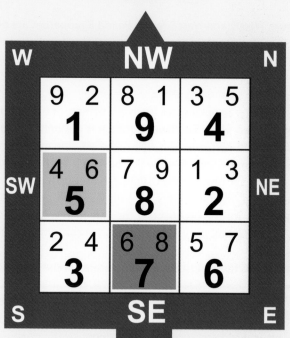

Facing NW1 (戌)

Where do you put your aquarium?

Best Location	Southeast
2ⁿᵈ Best Location	Southwest

Commentary

An aquarium in the Southeast will bring about overall positive wealth and career opportunities for the occupants of the household. However, this positive outcome may be more associated with the occupants being more contented and satisfied with their lot in life, than in terms of creating more opportunities to increase wealth or for career progression. As the effect of Water on this location is more on mental and emotional satisfaction, the 'feel good factor' over wealth and career issues comes from career and job satisfaction, as well as emotional contentment, rather than a material improvement in both these areas.

If the aquarium is located in the Southwest, it needs to be supported by External Formations to unlock its full potential. Where for example, an aquarium is located in the Southwest, and there is incoming Water or an incoming road at the Southwest, the "Receiving Early Heaven Water" Formation is considered to be perfected. In such a Formation, wealth comes from status, authority, power and recognition, as well as assistance from Noble People. So for example, this formation would benefit individuals in public service, or CEOs or upper management of large companies as these are people who have high status, ample power and authority, or significant public recognition.

In a Northwest 1 Period 8 property, we specifically do not want to have water present in the West, or have water exiting at the West sectors (such as a drain or river). This is a formation known as "Water Clashing Out Later Heaven".

This formation is particularly destructive financially, as it can bring about the loss of all family assets and property. Specifically, the loss of assets and property will be as a result of carelessness in legal responsibilities or obligations for example, or naivety of the occupants that results in them being defrauded of the family assets or property.

Northwest 2 (乾) or Northwest 3 (亥) Facing Homes in Period 8

NW2 (乾) / NW3 (亥)

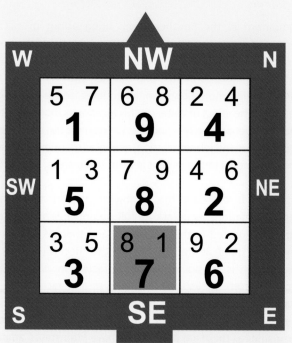

Where do you put your aquarium?

| Best Location | Southeast |

Commentary

With an aquarium in the Southeast sector, the occupants of a Northeast 2 or Northeast 3 Facing Period 8 property will benefit from overall prosperity. However, this water location is particularly beneficial from the standpoint of creating financial opportunities for those in academic, scholastic or creative fields. It is also highly beneficial for wealth opportunities if the occupants work in financial services or the financial industry, as well as those who engage in trading-based businesses or jobs that involve trading (including stocks and commodities).

However, the Water in this location should be contained so an aquarium is ideal. If you have a swimming pool in this location, make sure it is not an infinity pool as this is then classified as water 'leaving' the property at Southeast and the outcomes will be vastly different.

Like in the Northwest 1 facing Period 8 property, we do not want to have water present in the West sector or exiting at the West for a Northwest 2 or Northwest 3 facing Period 8 property. This is a negative Formation known as "Water Clashing Out Later Heaven" and denotes loss of wealth as a result of litigation, disputes or legal problems.

In addition, the Northwest 2/3 Facing Period 8 property should not have water present or placed in the Northwest sector. Admittedly, the #8 Facing Star is located in the Northwest, but placing Water in this location will violate the Direct/Indirect Spirit principle of the current period, which is Period 8. So whilst there will be immediate and possibly quick financial gains, these will be vastly overshadowed by long-term losses, and ultimately, significant financial setbacks and obstacles in the long-run. In addition, this negative formation has an adverse effect on the health of the occupants, and the family relationships of the occupants.

North 1 (壬) Facing Homes in Period 8

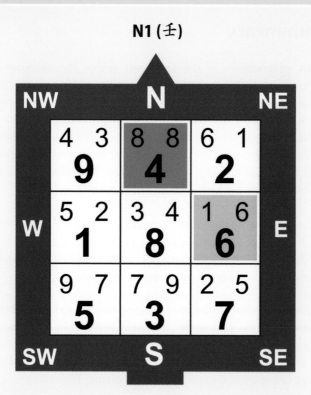

N1 (壬)

Where do you put your aquarium?

Best Location	North
2nd Best Location	East

Commentary

As far as possible, if you can match the location of the aquarium to your professional or personal needs, that is ideal. For example, in a North 1 Period 8 home, Water in the North is especially beneficial for those who work in heavy industries, or are involved in production lines or factories.

Matching the location of the aquarium to the professional or career needs of the members of the household however is quite a challenge in general for the average household where there may be several family members who are working. So realistically, this is only an option for a single occupant household or where only one occupant is working. Also, the key word here is 'ideal'. It does not mean that if no one in the household works in heavy industries, production or factory-linked jobs, activating the North with an aquarium brings zero benefits.

Water in the North for the North 1 Period 8 home brings about general wealth and prosperity (meaning, good health and high productivity, as well as positive family relationships) to all occupants of the household. Water in North also ensures the financial situation of the household are stable (long-term, steady growth in net worth, minimal loss of wealth) and there is low debt or no debt for most of the household members.

Although an aquarium in the East is regarded as the second best location for an aquarium, this location brings extra perks to those who are in professional fields such as lawyers, doctors, engineers and accountants. Water in the East in a North 1 Period 8 house is a formation known as "Receiving Later Heaven Water" – this is particularly suitable for professionals as the nature of the business is dependent on steady, consistent work, and smooth business operations with regular, consistent opportunities rather than one-off big deals.

North 2 (子) or North 3 (癸) Facing Homes in Period 8

N2 (子) / N3 (癸)

	N	
NW		NE
2 5 **9**	7 9 **4**	9 7 **2**
W 1 6 **1**	3 4 **8**	5 2 **6** E
6 1 **5**	8 8 **3**	4 3 **7**
SW	S	SE

Where do you put your aquarium?

Best Location	North
2nd Best Location	Southwest

Commentary

You will notice that in the North 2 and North 3 Period 8 homes, Water is also best located in the North, but this produces somewhat different outcomes compared to Water in the North for a North 1 Period 8 home. Whilst in both instances, it is favourable for wealth generation, Water in the North for a North 1 house generates steady financial growth. Whilst Water in the North for a North 2 and North 3 Period 8 home opens up investment opportunities as well. In Feng Shui terminology, an aquarium in the North of a North 1 house generates Direct Wealth opportunities, whilst Water in the North in a North 2/3 house generates both Direct and Indirect Wealth opportunities.

Water in the North in a North 2 /3 Period 8 home is specifically favourable for those in the entertainment, beauty, fashion and creative or design industries. If you are in any of these industries, Water in the North will enable you to achieve the break-through you need because it increases popularity, and peer support. For example, those in the entertainment industry will find they have more fans or more supporters. Those in the fashion industry may find their product becomes widely accepted or becomes a fashion 'must-have.'

Water in the Southwest of a North 2 or North 3 Period 8 house generates long-term wealth opportunities and promotes steady, long-term wealth advancement and growth. In such instance, the occupants will find that they need to be more patient with their expectations when it comes to their bank accountants. Water in the Southwest of a North 2 or North 3 Period 8 house is generally more supportive towards those in literary, academic or scholarly fields (such as those in R&D, or teaching or education) or those who have a career in sports. So for example, a tennis coach or golf pro living in a North 2 or North 3 Period 8 house should favour Water in the Southwest rather than Water in the North.

It is highly negative for North 2 or North 3 Period 8 homes to have water (be it internal or external) at the Northwest sector. This is a formation known as "Water Clashing Out Later Heaven" and is a highly ruinous formation. Not only does it cause a loss of wealth, but wealth accumulated through the generations of the family will also be lost.

Northeast 1 (䷑) Facing Homes in Period 8

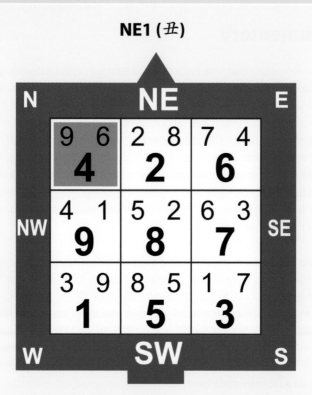

NE1 (䷑)

Where do you put your aquarium?

Best Location	North

Commentary

If only an aquarium is placed in the North in a Northeast 1 Period 8 home, then the occupants of the household can expect positive outcomes in terms of authority, status and power. Career employees will find they have a steady upwardly mobile career path and those who are self-employed or entrepreneurs will find they have no difficulty making a name for themselves or their business.

But for this placement of Water to be at its most effective, the layout of the property has to support a formation known as "Receiving Early Heaven Water." For the formation to be considered present, the aquarium must be located in the North and the North and Northwest sectors of the home must essentially be one large room. This means the Qi flows unobstructed from the North sector to the Northwest sector easily and without the presence of obstructions such as walls or doors. Alternatively, if there is a road coming in at the Northwest, and an aquarium in the North, then the "Receiving Early Heaven Water" formation is also fulfilled. In such instances when the Formation is considered present, there is not only strong recognition of the person, high status and a good reputation, but strong wealth opportunities will also arise.

If there is an open space (such as a field, or a garden or a balcony) at the Southeast sector of the home, or an incoming road entering from the Southeast sector, a different formation is in play when Water is located in the North. This is a formation known as "Receiving Later Heaven Water". This formation however requires that the Southeast and South sectors be one large room, or where Qi flow from the Southeast to the South sector is unobstructed by walls or doors. Where the Formation is present, the occupants of the property will enjoy excellent wealth and career opportunities, particularly if they are in sports or in a skill-based profession (ie: design, writing, carpentry, electrician).

Northeast 2 (艮) or Northeast 3 (寅) Facing Homes in Period 8

NE2 (艮) / NE3 (寅)

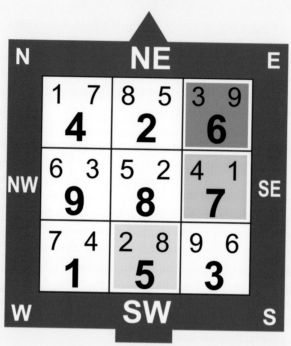

Where do you put your aquarium?

Best Location	East
2nd Best Location	Southeast
3rd Best Location	Southwest

Commentary

An aquarium in the East is the best location if a positive financial outcome is being sought. Water in this location not only brings about an increase in wealth, but opens up opportunities for the occupants to obtain wealth from multiple sources or creates multiple revenue streams. This is a suitable location for occupants who work in commission-based jobs such as sales, or those who are self-employed or entrepreneurs. In particular, entrepreneurs will have ample opportunities to expand their businesses and there will be investment opportunities abound as well.

An aquarium in the Southeast arguably is more beneficial if you are, for example, an author or a drug researcher. Locating Water here is specifically beneficial to the creation and generation of wealth opportunities that originates from academic, scholastic or creative endeavours. If you don't work in the academic, scholastic or creative industries, this Water location will still be helpful – you will have opportunities to achieve financial freedom or enhance your financial status through educational pursuits about financial matters. So for example, if you take an options trading course, and your home is a Northeast 2 or Northeast 3 Facing home in Period 8, you will be able to make use of the knowledge you have obtained to increase your wealth.

Assuming that you find you can only locate your aquarium in the Southwest, this is still a beneficial location for wealth opportunities. You will find you are more receptive to opportunities out there, especially those that are centered around residual income (such as collecting rental, or royalties). However, this location is preferred if a majority of the occupants are working professionals, rather than those who are self-employed or entrepreneurs.

East 1 (甲) Facing Homes in Period 8

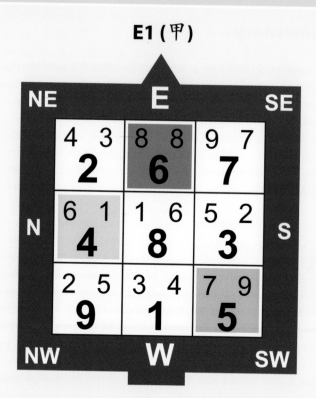

E1 (甲)

Where do you put your aquarium?

Best Location	East
2nd Best Location	Southwest
3rd Best Location	North

Commentary

As different stars are being activated when water is placed in different sectors in the home, the outcomes will also differ. For the East 1 Period 8 property, locating the aquarium in the East is favourable for both those who are in employment and those who are entrepreneurs. Water in this location ensures smooth sailing in career and entrepreneurial endeavours. (What does smooth sailing mean exactly? It could mean no ups and downs as well, meaning, progress is just average, but steady.)

If you are able to locate the aquarium in the Southwest, and your job scope involves sales or marketing, activating the stars here will be positive for your job as it fosters opportunities in networking and enhances communication skills. Locating your aquarium here is also positive for long-term wealth growth and investment. The key word here is long-term so your expectations should be on investment outcomes that take 5-10 years to reach profitability or maximum growth potential.

An aquarium in the North area is favourable if there are family members or occupants of the property who are engaged in literary or educational pursuits or jobs that involve literary skills such as writing or design. Children who are going to school and living in an East 1 Period 8 home with an aquarium at the North will excel well in both academic and ex-curricular activities, especially sports.

East 2 (卯) or East 3 (乙) Facing Homes in Period 8

E2 (卯) / E3 (乙)

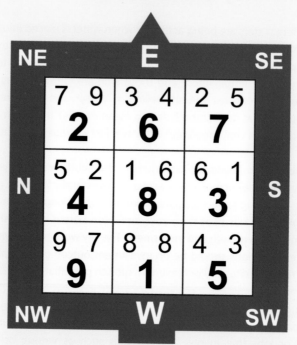

Where do you put your aquarium?

East 2 and East 3 Facing homes in Period 8 fall into a special category of Flying Star charts wherein the placement of water is not suitable. As such, a different approach has to be utilised to activate the Qi in the home, specifically an approach that DOES NOT involve the use of Water.

Commentary

Not only are East 2 and East 3 Period 8 Homes not suitable for the placement of water, but these homes also need to ensure there is NO WATER in the West sector. You might be wondering: why not? After all, isn't the Facing Star #8 in the West and won't I be activating those glorious 'Double 8s' by placing or having Water in the West? The placement of Water in the West is a violation of the Direct-Indirect Spirit Principle for the current period. So whilst placing water in the West and thus activating the Facing #8 will bring about some quick and fast gains initially, you'll find that ultimately and in the long-term, there is no ability to hold on to the wealth or worse, any gains made in the short-term are ultimately wiped out and debts are ultimately incurred instead.

In such properties, you will need to try to create or ensure there is an open space in a specific sector to activate the Qi. An open space includes an indoor garden with no roof, a large spacious living room or a balcony at this location if you live in a condominium or apartment. A spacious foyer in the area immediately outside the sector also qualifies as an open space in the sector for Qi to collect.

For East 2 and East 3 Facing homes in Period 8, you will need the open space area to be located in the Southwest sector or outside the Southwest sector. If you have a room in the Southwest sector, make sure that you are able to easily move from the Southwest sector to the West sector unencumbered – for example, the Southwest and West sector are one large spacious room OR the Southwest and West rooms are connected by a door or a short corridor. This set-up is favourable for investment opportunities of a short-term nature, and speculative investments.

As a general rule, it is unwise to opt for an East 2 or East 3 Facing Home in Period 8 due to these complications. This is especially the case if you are purchasing an apartment or condominium. If for some reason, you find yourself seriously considering purchasing an East 2 or East 3 Facing Period 8 property, I highly recommend getting a Feng Shui consultant to vet the property first to check the External Landforms or to help you get an idea of what kind of renovations or changes you may need to implement in order to wring some Feng Shui benefits out of the property.

Southeast 1 (辰) Facing Homes in Period 8

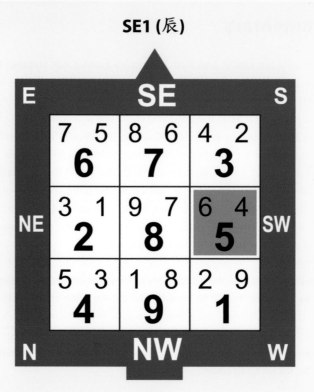

SE1 (辰)

E	SE	S
7 5 **6**	8 6 **7**	4 2 **3**
NE 3 1 **2**	9 7 **8**	6 4 **5** SW
5 3 **4**	1 8 **9**	2 9 **1**
N	NW	W

Where do you put your aquarium?

Best Location	Southwest 3 (232.6° – 247.5°)

Commentary

Overall, the Southeast 1 Period 8 property needs to use external water rather than internal water. If you intend to use internal water to activate the Qi, then you have to locate it EXACTLY in the Southwest 3 sector. You cannot simply place it in the Southwest sector generally.

Furthermore, an aquarium in the Southwest 3 location is generally more favourable to entrepreneurs and business owners, and less beneficial to those who are in the employ of others. When the aquarium is correctly located in the Southwest 3 sector, then partnerships and wheeling-dealing opportunities will arise, and there will be strong opportunities for business expansion. Entrepreneurs and business owners in industries with franchise opportunities (ie: food, software, technology) will particularly benefit if they are using a Southeast 1 Period 8 property, and can locate water at the Southwest 3 location.

For the Southeast 1 facing Period 8 property, it is important to ensure that there is no Water, either internally or externally, present in the South. There should also not be any water exiting at the South in the form of a drain, or an infinity pool. This is known as the "Water Clashing Out Early Heaven" formation and results in a loss of wealth or loss of revenue earning capacity as a result of poor health or health problems.

Southeast 2 (巽) or Southeast 3 (巳) Facing Homes in Period 8

SE2 (巽) / SE3 (巳)

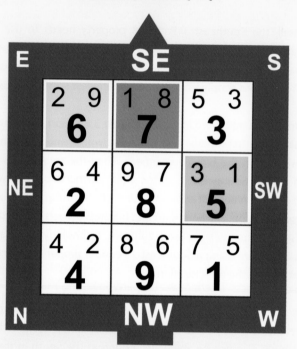

Where do you put your aquarium?

Best Location	Southeast
2nd Best Location	Southwest
3rd Best Location	East

Commentary

If the majority of the occupants of the property are self-employed professionals such as doctors, accountants, engineers or lawyers, or working in the employ of others as professionals, then try to locate the aquarium in the Southeast sector of the home. This water position will bring about strong career opportunities and also, recognition of abilities, for those in professional fields.

By contrast, the Southwest location water will be better if the main breadwinner or breadwinners are involved in academic fields such as teaching or education, or are engaged in scholarship such as research. This water location opens up opportunities in investments and increases opportunities to achieve financial freedom through prudent investing.

Those seeking to build their net worth through properties or looking to achieve financial freedom via property investing may want to favour locating the aquarium in the East rather than the other locations. The locating of Water in the East sector in a Southeast 2 or Southeast 3 facing Period 8 property is specifically conducive to an increase in assets and chattels or via property and land acquisition.

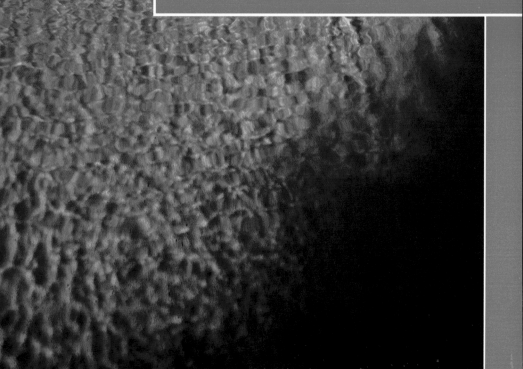

Chapter 7:
Tricks of the Water Trade

Tricks of the Water Trade

Here are a few important considerations to keep in mind when looking to use Water to activate the Qi in your home. I have discussed both External and Internal Water options here, but if at any point you feel uncertain, stick to the Internal – whilst you won't get super-duper results, you will certainly be certain of seeing measurable improvement without too much hassle and with relative ease.

Although throughout this book I have indicated the use of an aquarium to activate and collect Qi, it is not essential that you use an aquarium. You can use any kind of water receptacle or water feature you like, as long as it conforms to the size dimensions I have indicated. But I think you'll find that an aquarium really is just the most convenient means to achieve this aim and really just takes the judgment and guesswork out of the equation.

Use External Water where possible

If you live in landed property, space permitting, you may want to consider using External Water rather than Internal Water. External Water can be a swimming pool, a fish or koi pond, a fountain or simply a very large outdoor aquarium or just an open tank of water, if you are not too fussed about aesthetics.

As a general rule, swimming pools and fish ponds are preferred because they are generally quiet, and you don't have to worry about whether or not the water is splashing too much, or is too noisy. The water also tends to move slowly in a gentle circulating manner. Fountains on the other hand can be quite loud, or the water can gush too fiercely, resulting in Yang Water rather than Yin Water. As these require quite a bit of adjustment to get the right level, they add complexity to the task.

If you intend to install a fish pond or swimming pool to serve as your External Water, remember, shallow water is not as productive and effective. Make sure your fish pond or swimming pool is of a reasonable depth. 2-3 feet is a good minimum depth.

Remember to locate the External Water in the sector that is indicated as suitable for your home. External is of course not an option generally for individuals living in landed property with very little open space (such as link houses) and for those living in apartments. In these instances, use Internal Water.

All you need to know about Internal Water Features

There are water features, and there are water features!

As a rule, any Internal Water feature must take into account the following considerations:

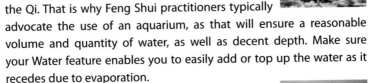

- **Size and Depth matters** - Shallow and small receptacles generally do not work well to activate the Qi. That is why Feng Shui practitioners typically advocate the use of an aquarium, as that will ensure a reasonable volume and quantity of water, as well as decent depth. Make sure your Water feature enables you to easily add or top up the water as it recedes due to evaporation.

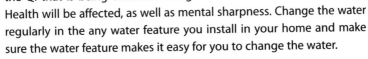

- **Easy to keep clean** - Cloudy, dirty and foul-smelling water is considered Sha Qi water and results in the Qi that is being collected being contaminated. Health will be affected, as well as mental sharpness. Change the water regularly in the any water feature you install in your home and make sure the water feature makes it easy for you to change the water.

- **Exposed surface area** - For Qi to collect, the water must be visible and exposed. If you are using an aquarium, leave the top open so that the water can be seen. If you are just using a large receptacle, make sure again the surface of the water is visible.

I have found that the best Internal Water features are actually the easy (and cheap!) ones. Some of the best options for Internal Water include the following:

- Aquariums - As a rule of thumb, for any property between 800-1000 square feet would need an aquarium that is a minimum size of 3 feet by 3 feet. A larger property accordingly would need a bigger tank. A cheap, and pleasant option.

- Water Towers – have the added advantage of being very portable (convenient for those who are looking to activate Monthly Stars). These work because they have depth, and generally also require a fair amount of water in them to work effectively. They are also generally quite innocent looking and do not attract 'Feng Shui suspicion'! However, these are generally only good for spaces under 500 square feet.

- A large urn or receptacle of water – not very pretty but does the job! Also unlikely to be noisy so no risk of accidentally landing up with Yang Water. Make sure it is deep, with a large 'mouth' so that there is enough water surface exposed.

By contrast, the fancy-schmancy, expensive and pretty 'Water features' are the worst options! The following are some common examples of popular so-called Water features, which in my view, are not very effective if you want to activate and collect Qi in your home.

- Tabletop Fountains – these are quite popular and widely available in many themes and motifs. Unfortunately, they are too small to actually have any effect because they usually do not contain very much water. Qi needs a decent body of Water to collect and gather at

otherwise, let's face it, your bedside water glass could collect Qi and the puddles in your garden would collect Qi. Remember the key to any good Water feature is depth, size and volume of water.

- Wheeled or Tiered Indoor Fountains – as a general rule, I do not encourage the use of such fountains because they rarely contain more than a few cups of water. These fountains are also usually designed to be placed on top of desks or small side tables, which usually  means they are not of a sufficient size to actually enable the meaningful collection of Qi. As a guide, if you are putting no more than 1.5 litres of water into your fountain, it's too small and not effective in the least.

- Crying Walls – this is quite popular in hotels although slowly, it is becoming a common aesthetic feature in some architecturally modern homes. A crying wall is like a horizontal river – water runs down the side of the wall, usually into an invisible drain underneath. The 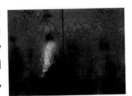 problem with crying walls is that the water neither collects or pools (since it typically goes straight into a drain and back up round the back to run down the wall again) nor is there any real depth in the area where the water does collect or pool. Furthermore, the collection point of the water is likely to be invisible to the eye for aesthetic purposes, which means the water surface is not visible. Qi cannot gather if the surface of the Water is not visible. As such, crying walls are not effective as a Water feature.

- A Vase of Water – as a general rule of thumb, if your vase cannot hold 3 litres of water in it, then it's not doing much for the Qi in your house. A normal flower vase does not usually hold enough water or have a wide enough surface area to be effective for the purposes  of activating Qi. A vase is typically more useful if you want to activate a particular Flying Star, such as the #4. But to collect and activate Qi within a home, it's not effective. Remember, size, volume and depth!

Install your aquarium on an auspicious date

This is particularly important if you have to use Internal Water. Since you are already slightly disadvantaged, all the more you want to make sure you maximise the outcome of installing your aquarium by using a good date.

For the installation of an aquarium or Water feature, typically, you should select a date that satisfies the following criteria:

- Select a Success or Open Day if you are using the 12 Officers system. Make sure that the Branch of the Day does not clash with the Branch of your Year Pillar in your BaZi. So for example, if you are born in the year of the Snake, do not select a Pig Day that is also a Success or Open Day.

For those with some knowledge of Date Selection or who have read my book *The Art of Date Selection: Personal Date Selection*, you can take it a step further.

- Select a Success or Open Day according to the 12 Officers system. Ensure the Branch of the Day does not clash your Year Pillar Branch.

- The Success or Open Day should contain your Wealth Element, as dictated by your BaZi, on the Stem. This will ensure that installing the aquarium on that date does bring wealth.

- Use only Success or Open Days which satisfy the above criteria, which are also Superior Days, according to the Dong Gong System.

About Joey Yap

Joey Yap is the founder of the Mastery Academy of Chinese Metaphysics, a global organization devoted to the teaching of Feng Shui, BaZi, Mian Xiang and other Chinese Metaphysics subjects. He is also the Chief Consultant of Yap Global Consulting, an international consulting firm specialising in Feng Shui and Chinese Astrology services and audits.

Joey Yap is the bestselling author of over 30 books on Feng Shui, Chinese Astrology, Face Reading and Yi Jing, many of which have topped the Malaysian and Singaporean MPH bookstores' bestseller lists.

Thousands of students from all around the world have learnt and mastered Classical Feng Shui, Chinese Astrology, and other Chinese Metaphysics subjects through Joey Yap's structured learning programs, books and online training. Joey Yap's courses are currently taught by over 30 instructors worldwide.

Every year Joey Yap conducts his 'Feng Shui and Astrology' seminar to a crowd of more than 3500 people at the Kuala Lumpur Convention Center. He also takes this annual seminar on a world tour to Frankfurt, San Francisco, New York, Toronto, London, Sydney and Singapore.

In addition to being a regular guest on various radio and TV shows, Joey Yap has also written columns for The New Straits Times and The Star - Malaysia's two leading newspapers. He has also been featured in many popular global publications and networks like Time International, Forbes International, the International Herald Tribune and Bloomberg.

He has also hosted his own TV series, 'Discover Feng Shui with Joey Yap', on 8TV, a local Malaysian network in 2005; and 'Walking The Dragons with Joey Yap' on Astro Wah Lai Toi, Malaysia's cable network in 2008.

Joey Yap has worked with HSBC, Bloomberg, Microsoft, Samsung, IBM, HP, Alliance, Great Eastern, Citibank, Standard Chartered, OCBC, SIME UEP, Mah Sing, Auto Bavaria, Volvo, AXA, Singtel, ABN Amro, CIMB, Hong-Leong, Manulife and others.

Author's personal website :www.joeyyap.com

Follow Joey Yap's regular updates on Twitter:

 www.twitter.com/joeyyap

Join Joey Yap on Facebook:

 www.facebook.com/JoeyYapFB

EDUCATION
The Mastery Academy of Chinese Metaphysics:
the first choice for practitioners and aspiring students of the art and science of Chinese Classical Feng Shui and Astrology.

For thousands of years, Eastern knowledge has been passed from one generation to another through the system of discipleship. A venerated master would accept suitable individuals at a young age as his disciples, and informally through the years, pass on his knowledge and skills to them. His disciples in turn, would take on their own disciples, as a means to perpetuate knowledge or skills.

This system served the purpose of restricting the transfer of knowledge to only worthy honourable individuals and ensuring that outsiders or Westerners would not have access to thousands of years of Eastern knowledge, learning and research.

However, the disciple system has also resulted in Chinese Metaphysics and Classical Studies lacking systematic teaching methods. Knowledge garnered over the years has not been accumulated in a concise, systematic manner, but scattered amongst practitioners, each practicing his/her knowledge, art and science, in isolation.

The disciple system, out of place in today's modern world, endangers the advancement of these classical fields that continue to have great relevance and application today.

At the Mastery Academy of Chinese Metaphysics, our Mission is to bring Eastern Classical knowledge in the fields of metaphysics, Feng Shui and Astrology sciences and the arts to the world. These Classical teachings and knowledge, previously shrouded in secrecy and passed on only through the discipleship system, are adapted into structured learning, which can easily be understood, learnt and mastered. Through modern learning methods, these renowned ancient arts, sciences and practices can be perpetuated while facilitating more extensive application and understanding of these classical subjects.

The Mastery Academy espouses an educational philosophy that draws from the best of the East and West. It is the world's premier educational institution for the study of Chinese Metaphysics Studies offering a wide range and variety of courses, ensuring that students have the opportunity to pursue their preferred field of study and enabling existing practitioners and professionals to gain cross-disciplinary knowledge that complements their current field of practice.

Courses at the Mastery Academy have been carefully designed to ensure a comprehensive yet compact syllabus. The modular nature of the courses enables students to immediately begin to put their knowledge into practice while pursuing continued study of their field and complementary fields. Students thus have the benefit of developing and gaining practical experience in tandem with the expansion and advancement of their theoretical knowledge.

Students can also choose from a variety of study options, from a distance learning program, the Homestudy Series, that enables study at one's own pace or intensive foundation courses and compact lecture-based courses, held in various cities around the world by Joey Yap or our licensed instructors. The Mastery Academy's faculty and make-up is international in nature, thus ensuring that prospective students can attend courses at destinations nearest to their country of origin or with a licensed Mastery Academy instructor in their home country.

The Mastery Academy provides 24x7 support to students through its Online Community, with a variety of tools, documents, forums and e-learning materials to help students stay at the forefront of research in their fields and gain invaluable assistance from peers and mentoring from their instructors.

TM

MASTERY ACADEMY
OF CHINESE METAPHYSICS

www.masteryacademy.com

MALAYSIA
19-3, The Boulevard
Mid Valley City
59200 Kuala Lumpur, Malaysia
Tel : +603-2284 8080
Fax : +603-2284 1218
Email : info@masteryacademy.com

Australia, Austria, Canada, China, Croatia, Cyprus, Czech Republic, Denmark, France, Germany, Greece, Hungary, India, Italy, Kazakhstan, Malaysia, Netherlands (Holland), New Zealand, Philippines, Poland, Russian Federation, Singapore, Slovenia, South Africa, Switzerland, Turkey, U.S.A., Ukraine, United Kingdom

Introducing...
The Mastery Academy's E-Learning Center!

The Mastery Academy's goal has always been to share authentic knowledge of Chinese Metaphysics with the whole world.

Nevertheless, we do recognize that distance, time, and hotel and traveling costs – amongst many other factors – could actually hinder people from enrolling for a classroom-based course. But with the advent and amazing advance of IT today, NOT any more!

With this in mind, we have invested heavily in IT, to conceive what is probably the first and only E-Learning Center in the world today that offers a full range of studies in the field of Chinese Metaphysics.

Convenient   Study from Your   Easy Enrollment
                    Own Home

The Mastery Academy's E-Learning Center

Now, armed with your trusty computer or laptop, and Internet access, knowledge of classical Feng Shui, BaZi (Destiny Analysis) and Mian Xiang (Face Reading) are but a literal click away!

Study at your own pace, and interact with your Instructor and fellow students worldwide, from anywhere in the world. With our E-Learning Center, knowledge of Chinese Metaphysics is brought DIRECTLY to you in all its clarity – topic-by-topic, and lesson-by-lesson; with illustrated presentations and comprehensive notes expediting your learning curve!

Your education journey through our E-Learning Center may be done via any of the following approaches:

1. Online Courses

There are 3 Programs available: our Online Feng Shui Program, Online BaZi Program, and Online Mian Xiang Program. Each Program consists of several Levels, with each Level consisting of many Lessons in turn. Each Lesson contains a pre-recorded video session on the topic at hand, accompanied by presentation-slides and graphics as well as downloadable tutorial notes that you can print and file for future reference.

Video Lecture

Presentation Slide

Downloadable Notes

2. MA Live!

MA Live!, as its name implies, enables LIVE broadcasts of Joey Yap's courses and seminars – right to your computer screen. Students will not only get to see and hear Joey talk on real-time 'live', but also participate and more importantly, TALK to Joey via the MA Live! interface. All the benefits of a live class, minus the hassle of actually having to attend one!

How It Works   1.

2.

Our Live Classes   You at Home

3. Video-On-Demand (VOD)

Get immediate streaming-downloads of the Mastery Academy's wide range of educational DVDs, right on your computer screen. No more shipping costs and waiting time to be incurred!

Instant VOD Online   1.

2.

Choose From Our list   Click "Play" on Your PC
of Available VODs!

Welcome to **www.maelearning.com**; the web portal of our E-Learning Center, and YOUR virtual gateway to Chinese Metaphysics!

Mastery Academy around the world

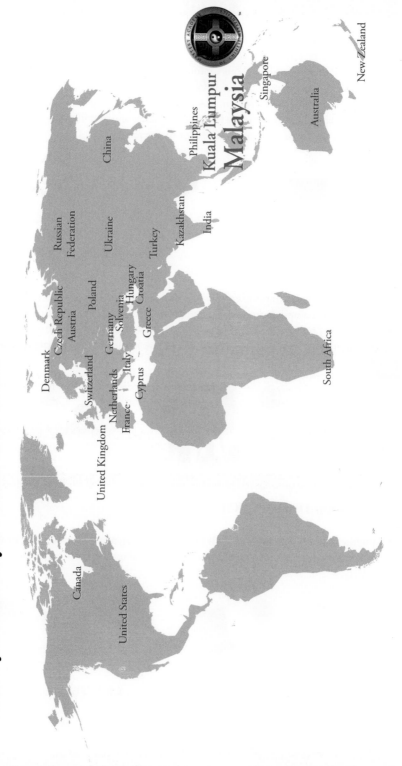

Canada
United States
United Kingdom
Denmark
Czech Republic
Austria
Switzerland
Poland
Netherlands
Germany
Solvenia
Hungary
France
Italy
Croatia
Cyprus
Greece
Russian Federation
Ukraine
Turkey
Kazakhstan
China
India
Philippines
Kuala Lumpur
Malaysia
Singapore
South Africa
Australia
New Zealand

YAP GLOBAL CONSULTING

Joey Yap & Yap Global Consulting

Headed by Joey Yap, Yap Global Consulting (YGC) is a leading international consulting firm specializing in Feng Shui, Mian Xiang (Face Reading) and BaZi (Destiny Analysis) consulting services worldwide. Joey Yap - an internationally renowned Master Trainer, Consultant, Speaker and best-selling Author - has dedicated his life to the art and science of Chinese Metaphysics.

YGC has its main office in Kuala Lumpur, and draws upon its diverse reservoir of strength from a group of dedicated and experienced consultants based in more than 30 countries, worldwide.

As the pioneer in blending established, classical Chinese Metaphysics techniques with the latest approach in consultation practices, YGC has built its reputation on the principles of professionalism and only the highest standards of service. This allows us to retain the cutting edge in delivering Feng Shui and Destiny consultation services to both corporate and personal clients, in a simple and direct manner, without compromising on quality.

Across Industries: Our Portfolio of Clients

Our diverse portfolio of both corporate and individual clients from all around the world bears testimony to our experience and capabilities.

Virtually every industry imaginable has benefited from our services - ranging from academic and financial institutions, real-estate developers and multinational corporations, to those in the leisure and tourism industry. Our services are also engaged by professionals, prominent business personalities, celebrities, high-profile politicians and people from all walks of life.

YAP GLOBAL CONSULTING

Name (Mr./Mrs./Ms.):_____

Contact Details

Tel:_____ Fax:_____

Mobile :_____

E-mail:_____

What Type of Consultation Are You Interested In?
☐ Feng Shui   ☐ BaZi   ☐ Date Selection   ☐ Yi Jing

Please tick if applicable:
☐ Are you a Property Developer looking to engage Yap Global Consulting?

☐ Are you a Property Investor looking for tailor-made packages to suit your investment requirements?

Please attach your name card here.

Thank you for completing this form. Please fax it back to us at:

Malaysia & the rest of the world
Fax : +603-2284 2213   Tel : +603-2284 1213

Feng Shui Consultations

For Residential Properties
- Initial Land/Property Assessment
- Residential Feng Shui Consultations
- Residential Land Selection
- End-to-End Residential Consultation

For Commercial Properties
- Initial Land/Property Assessment
- Commercial Feng Shui Consultations
- Commercial Land Selection
- End-to-End Commercial Consultation

For Property Developers
- End-to-End Consultation
- Post-Consultation Advisory Services
- Panel Feng Shui Consultant

For Property Investors
- Your Personal Feng Shui Consultant
- Tailor-Made Packages

For Memorial Parks & Burial Sites
- Yin House Feng Shui

BaZi Consultations

Personal Destiny Analysis
- Personal Destiny Analysis for Individuals
- Children's BaZi Analysis
- Family BaZi Analysis

Strategic Analysis for Corporate Organizations
- Corporate BaZi Consultations
- BaZi Analysis for Human Resource Management

Entrepreneurs & Business Owners
- BaZi Analysis for Entrepreneurs

Career Pursuits
- BaZi Career Analysis

Relationships
- Marriage and Compatibility Analysis
- Partnership Analysis

For Everyone
- Annual BaZi Forecast
- Your Personal BaZi Coach

Date Selection Consultations

- **Marriage Date Selection**
- **Caesarean Birth Date Selection**
- **House-Moving Date Selection**
- **Renovation & Groundbreaking Dates**

- **Signing of Contracts**
- **Official Openings**
- **Product Launches**

Yi Jing Assessment

A Time-Tested, Accurate Science

- With a history predating 4 millennia, the Yi Jing - or Classic of Change - is one of the oldest Chinese texts surviving today. Its purpose as an oracle, in predicting the outcome of things, is based on the variables of Time, Space and Specific Events.

- A Yi Jing Assessment provides specific answers to any specific questions you may have about a specific event or endeavor. This is something that a Destiny Analysis would not be able to give you.

Basically, what a Yi Jing Assessment does is focus on only ONE aspect or item at a particular point in your life, and give you a calculated prediction of the details that will follow suit, if you undertake a particular action. It gives you an insight into a situation, and what course of action to take in order to arrive at a satisfactory outcome at the end of the day.

Please Contact YGC for a personalized Yi Jing Assessment!

INVITING US TO YOUR CORPORATE EVENTS

Many reputable organizations and institutions have worked closely with YGC to build a synergistic business relationship by engaging our team of consultants, led by Joey Yap, as speakers at their corporate events. Our seminars and short talks are always packed with audiences consisting of clients and associates of multinational and public-listed companies as well as key stakeholders of financial institutions.

We tailor our seminars and talks to suit the anticipated or pertinent group of audience. Be it a department, subsidiary, your clients or even the entire corporation, we aim to fit your requirements in delivering the intended message(s).

Tel: +603-2284 1213   Email: consultation@joeyyap.com

CHINESE METAPHYSICS REFERENCE SERIES

The Chinese Metaphysics Reference Series is a collection of reference texts, source material, and educational textbooks to be used as supplementary guides by scholars, students, researchers, teachers and practitioners of Chinese Metaphysics.

These comprehensive and structured books provide fast, easy reference to aid in the study and practice of various Chinese Metaphysics subjects including Feng Shui, BaZi, Yi Jing, Zi Wei, Liu Ren, Ze Ri, Ta Yi, Qi Men and Mian Xiang.

The Chinese Metaphysics Compendium

At over 1,000 pages, the *Chinese Metaphysics Compendium* is a unique one-volume reference book that compiles all the formulas relating to Feng Shui, BaZi (Four Pillars of Destiny), Zi Wei (Purple Star Astrology), Yi Jing (I-Ching), Qi Men (Mystical Doorways), Ze Ri (Date Selection), Mian Xiang (Face Reading) and other sources of Chinese Metaphysics.

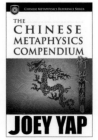

It is presented in the form of easy-to-read tables, diagrams and reference charts, all of which are compiled into one handy book. This first-of-its-kind compendium is presented in both English and the original Chinese, so that none of the meanings and contexts of the technical terminologies are lost.

The only essential and comprehensive reference on Chinese Metaphysics, and an absolute must-have for all students, scholars, and practitioners of Chinese Metaphysics.

The Ten Thousand Year Calendar

Dong Gong Date Selection

The Date Selection Compendium

Plum Blossoms Divination Reference Book

San Yuan Dragon Gate Eight Formations Water Method

Xuan Kong Da Gua Ten Thousand Year Calendar

Xuan Kong Da Gua Structures Reference Book

Xuan Kong Da Gua 64 Gua Transformation Analysis

Xuan Kong Purple White Script

Earth Study Discern Truth Second Edition

Bazi Structures and Structural Useful Gods - Wood

Bazi Structures and Structural Useful Gods - Fire

Bazi Structures and Structural Useful Gods - Earth

Bazi Structures and Structural Useful Gods - Metal

Bazi Structures and Structural Useful Gods - Water

Educational Tools & Software

Xuan Kong Flying Stars Feng Shui Software
The Essential Application for Enthusiasts and Professionals

The Xuan Kong Flying Stars Feng Shui Software is a brand-new application by Joey Yap that will assist you in the practice of Xuan Kong Feng Shui with minimum fuss and maximum effectiveness. Superimpose the Flying Stars charts over your house plans (or those of your clients) to clearly demarcate the 9 Palaces. Use it to help you create fast and sophisticated chart drawings and presentations, as well as to assist professional practitioners in the report-writing process before presenting the final reports for your clients. Students can use it to practice their Xuan Kong Feng Shui skills and knowledge, and it can even be used by designers and architects!

Some of the highlights of the software include:
- Natal Flying Stars
- Monthly Flying Stars
- 81 Flying Stars Combinations
- Dual-View Format
- Annual Flying Stars
- Flying Stars Integration
- 24 Mountains

All charts will be are printable and configurable, and can be saved for future editing. Also, you'll be able to export your charts into most image file formats like jpeg, bmp, and gif.

The Xuan Kong Flying Stars Feng Shui Software can make your Feng Shui practice simpler and more effective, garnering you amazing results with less effort!

Mini Feng Shui Compass

This Mini Feng Shui Compass with the accompanying Companion Booklet written by leading Feng Shui and Chinese Astrology Master Trainer Joey Yap is a must-have for any Feng Shui enthusiast.

The Mini Feng Shui Compass is a self-aligning compass that is not only light at 100gms but also built sturdily to ensure it will be convenient to use anywhere. The rings on the Mini Feng Shui Compass are bilingual and incorporate the 24 Mountain Rings that is used in your traditional Luo Pan.

The comprehensive booklet included will guide you in applying the 24 Mountain Directions on your Mini Feng Shui Compass effectively and the 8 Mansions Feng Shui to locate the most auspicious locations within your home, office and surroundings. You can also use the Mini Feng Shui Compass when measuring the direction of your property for the purpose of applying Flying Stars Feng Shui.

Educational Tools & Software

BaZi Ming Pan Software Version 2.0
Professional Four Pillars Calculator for Destiny Analysis

The BaZi Ming Pan Version 2.0 Professional Four Pillars Calculator for Destiny Analysis is the most technically advanced software of its kind in the world today. It allows even those without any knowledge of BaZi to generate their own BaZi Charts, and provides virtually every detail required to undertake a comprehensive Destiny Analysis.

This Professional Four Pillars Calculator allows you to even undertake a day-to-day analysis of your Destiny. What's more, all BaZi Charts generated by this software are fully printable and configurable! Designed for both enthusiasts and professional practitioners, this state-of-the-art software blends details with simplicity, and is capable of generating 4 different types of BaZi charts: **BaZi Professional Charts, BaZi Annual Analysis Charts, BaZi Pillar Analysis Charts and BaZi Family Relationship Charts.**

Additional references, configurable to cater to all levels of BaZi knowledge and usage, include:
• Dual Age & Bilingual Option (Western & Chinese) • Na Yin narrations • 12 Life Stages evaluation • Death & Emptiness • Gods & Killings • Special Days • Heavenly Virtue Nobles

This software also comes with a Client Management feature that allows you to save and trace clients' records instantly, navigate effortlessly between BaZi charts, and file your clients' information in an organized manner.

The BaZi Ming Pan Version 2.0 Calculator sets a new standard by combining the best of BaZi and technology.

Joey Yap Feng Shui Template Set

Directions are the cornerstone of any successful Feng Shui audit or application. The **Joey Yap Feng Shui Template Set** is a set of three templates to simplify the process of taking directions and determining locations and positions, whether it's for a building, a house, or an open area such as a plot of land, all with just a floor plan or area map.

The Set comprises 3 basic templates: The Basic Feng Shui Template, 8 Mansions Feng Shui Template, and the Flying Stars Feng Shui Template.

With bi-lingual notations for these directions; both in English and the original Chinese, the **Joey Yap Feng Shui Template Set** comes with its own Booklet that gives simple yet detailed instructions on how to make use of the 3 templates within.

• Easy-to-use, simple, and straightforward
• Small and portable; each template measuring only 5" x 5"
• Additional 8 Mansions and Flying Stars Reference Rings
• Handy companion booklet with usage tips and examples

Accelerate Your Face Reading Skills With Joey Yap's Face Reading Revealed DVD Series

Mian Xiang, the Chinese art of Face Reading, is an ancient form of physiognomy and entails the use of the face and facial characteristics to evaluate key aspects of a person's life, luck and destiny. In his Face Reading DVDs series, Joey Yap shows you how the facial features reveal a wealth of information about a person's luck, destiny and personality.

Mian Xiang also tell us the talents, quirks and personality of an individual. Do you know that just by looking at a person's face, you can ascertain his or her health, wealth, relationships and career? Let Joey Yap show you how the 12 Palaces can be utilised to reveal a person's inner talents, characteristics and much more.

Each facial feature on the face represents one year in a person's life. Your face is a 100-year map of your life and each position reveals your fortune and destiny at a particular age as well as insights and information about your personality, skills, abilities and destiny.

Using Mian Xiang, you will also be able to plan your life ahead by identifying, for example, the right business partner and knowing the sort of person that you need to avoid. By knowing their characteristics through the facial features, you will be able to gauge their intentions and gain an upper hand in negotiations.

Do you know what moles signify? Do they bring good or bad luck? Do you want to build better relationships with your partner or family members or have your ever wondered why you seem to be always bogged down by trivial problems in your life?

In these highly entertaining DVDs, Joey will help you answer all these questions and more. You will be able to ascertain the underlying meaning of moles, birthmarks or even the type of your hair in Face Reading. Joey will also reveal the guidelines to help you foster better and stronger relationships with your loved ones through Mian Xiang.

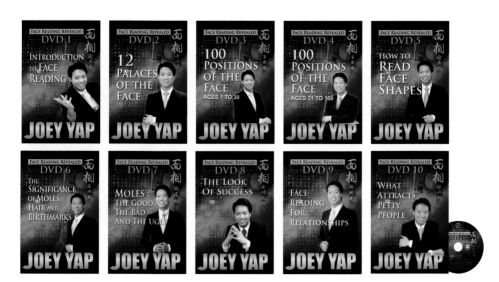

Feng Shui for Homebuyers DVD Series

Best-selling Author, and international Master Trainer and Consultant Joey Yap reveals in these DVDs the significant Feng Shui features that every homebuyer should know when evaluating a property.

Joey will guide you on how to customise your home to maximise the Feng Shui potential of your property and gain the full benefit of improving your health, wealth and love life using the 9 Palace Grid. He will show you how to go about applying the classical applications of the Life Gua and House Gua techniques to get attuned to your Sheng Qi (positive energies).

In these DVDs, you will also learn how to identify properties with good Feng Shui features that will help you promote a fulfilling life and achieve your full potential. Discover how to avoid properties with negative Feng Shui that can bring about detrimental effects to your health, wealth and relationships.

Joey will also elaborate on how to fix the various aspects of your home that may have an impact on the Feng Shui of your property and give pointers on how to tap into the positive energies to support your goals.

Discover Feng Shui with Joey Yap (TV Series)

Discover Feng Shui with Joey Yap: Set of 4 DVDs

Informative and entertaining, classical Feng Shui comes alive in *Discover Feng Shui with Joey Yap!*

Dying to know how you can use Feng Shui to improve your house or office, but simply too busy attend for formal classes?

You have the questions. Now let Joey personally answer them in this 4-set DVD compilation! Learn how to ensure the viability of your residence or workplace, Feng Shui-wise, without having to convert it into a Chinese antiques' shop. Classical Feng Shui is about harnessing the natural power of your environment to improve quality of life. It's a systematic and subtle metaphysical science.

And that's not all. Joey also debunks many a myth about classical Feng Shui, and shares with viewers Face Reading tips as well!

Own the series that national channel 8TV did a re-run of in 2005, today!

Continue Your Journey with Joey Yap's Books

Pure Feng Shui

Pure Feng Shui is Joey Yap's debut with an international publisher, CICO Books, and is a refreshing and elegant look at the intricacies of Classical Feng Shui – now compiled in a useful manner for modern-day readers. This book is a comprehensive introduction to all the important precepts and techniques of Feng Shui practice.

He reveals how to use Feng Shui to bring prosperity, good relationships, and success into one's life the simple and genuine way – without having to resort to symbols or figurines! He shows readers how to work with what they have and make simple and sustainable changes that can have significant Feng Shui effect. The principles of Classical Feng Shui and Chinese Astrology inform his teachings and explanations, so all that the readers need are a compass, a pencil, some paper, and an open mind!

Joey Yap's Art of Face Reading

The Art of Face Reading is Joey Yap's second effort with CICO Books, and takes a lighter, more practical approach to Face Reading. This book does not so much focus on the individual features as it does on reading the entire face. It is about identifying common personality types and characters.

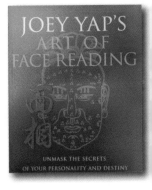

Joey shows readers how to identify successful career faces, or faces that are most likely to be able to do well financially. He also explores Face Reading in the context of health. He uses examples of real people - famous and ordinary folk - to allow readers to better understand what these facial features look like on an actual face. Readers will learn how to identify faces in Career, Wealth, Relationships, and Health (eg. 'The Salesperson Face,' 'The Politician Face,' 'The Unfaithful One,' 'The Shopaholic One,' and plenty more.)

Continue Your Journey with Joey Yap's Books

Easy Guide on Face Reading (English & Chinese versions)

The Face Reading Essentials series of books comprise 5 individual books on the key features of the face – Eyes, Eyebrows, Ears, Nose, and Mouth. Each book provides a detailed illustration and a simple yet descriptive explanation on the individual types of the features.

The books are equally useful and effective for beginners, enthusiasts, and the curious. The series is designed to enable people who are new to Face Reading to make the most of first impressions and learn to apply Face Reading skills to understand the personality and character of friends, family, co-workers, and even business associates.

 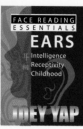 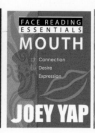 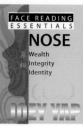 

BaZi Essentials Series (English & Chinese versions)

The BaZi Essentials series of books comprise 10 individual books that focus on the individual Day Masters in BaZi (Four Pillars of Destiny, or Chinese Astrology) study and analysis. With each book focusing on one particular Day Master, Joey explains why the Day Master is the fundamental starting point for BaZi analysis, and is the true essence of one's character traits and basic identity.

With these concise and entertaining books that are designed to be both informative and entertaining, Joey shows how each person is different and unique, yet share similar traits, according to his or her respective Day Master. These 10 guides will provide crucial insight into why people behave in the various different ways they do.

 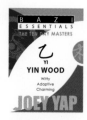   

Continue Your Journey with Joey Yap's Books

Walking the Dragons

Walking the Dragons is a guided tour through the classical landform Feng Shui of ancient China, an enchanting collection of deeply-researched yet entertaining essays rich in historical detail.

Compiled in one book for the first time from Joey Yap's Feng Shui Mastery Excursion Series, the book highlights China's extensive, vibrant history with astute observations on the Feng Shui of important sites and places. Learn the landform formations of Yin Houses (tombs and burial places), as well as mountains, temples, castles, and villages.

It demonstrates complex Feng Shui theories and principles in easy-to-understand, entertaining language and is the perfect addition to the bookshelf of a Feng Shui or history lover. Anyone, whether experienced in Feng Shui or new to the practice, will be able to enjoy the insights shared in this book. Complete with gorgeous full-colour pictures of all the amazing sights and scenery, it's the next best thing to having been there yourself!

Your Aquarium Here

Your Aquarium Here is a simple, practical, hands-on Feng Shui book that teaches you how to incorporate a Water feature – an aquarium – for optimal Feng Shui benefit, whether for personal relationships, wealth, or career. Designed to be comprehensive yet simple enough for a novice or beginner, *Your Aquarium Here* provides historical and factual information about the role of Water in Feng Shui, and provides a step-by-step guide to installing and using an aquarium.

The book is the first in the **Fengshuilogy Series**, a series of matter-of-fact and useful Feng Shui books designed for the person who wants to do fuss-free Feng Shui. Not everyone who wants to use Feng Shui is an expert or a scholar! This series of books are just the kind you'd want on your bookshelf to gain basic, practical knowledge of the subject. Go ahead and Feng Shui-It-Yourself – *Your Aquarium Here* eliminates all the fuss and bother, but maintains all the fun and excitement, of authentic Feng Shui application!

The Art of Date Selection: Personal Date Selection

In today's modern world, it is not good enough to just do things effectively – we need to do them efficiently, as well. From the signing of business contracts and moving into a new home, to launching a product or even tying the knot; everything has to move, and move very quickly too. There is a premium on Time, where mistakes can indeed be costly.

The notion of doing the Right Thing, at the Right Time and in the Right Place is the very backbone of Date Selection. Because by selecting a suitable date specially tailored to a specific activity or endeavor, we infuse it with the most positive energies prevalent in our environment during that particular point in time; and that could well make the difference between `make-and-break'! With the *Art of Date Selection: Personal Date Selection*, learn simple, practical methods you can employ to select not just good dates, but personalized good dates. Whether it's a personal activity such as a marriage or professional endeavor such as launching a business, signing a contract or even acquiring assets, this book will show you how to pick the good dates and tailor them to suit the activity in question, as well as avoid the negative ones too!

The Art of Date Selection: Feng Shui Date Selection

Date Selection is the Art of selecting the most suitable date, where the energies present on the day support the specific activities or endeavors we choose to undertake on that day. Feng Shui is the Chinese Metaphysical study of the Physiognomy of the Land – landforms and the Qi they produce, circulate and conduct. Hence, anything that exists on this Earth is invariably subject to the laws of Feng Shui. So what do we get when Date Selection and Feng Shui converge?

Feng Shui Date Selection, of course! Say you wish to renovate your home, or maybe buy or rent one. Or perhaps, you're a developer, and wish to know WHEN is the best date possible to commence construction works on your project. In any case – and all cases – you certainly wish to ensure that your endeavors are well supported by the positive energies present on a good day, won't you? And this is where Date Selection supplements the practice of Feng Shui. At the end of the day, it's all about making the most of what's good, and minimizing what's bad.

(Available Soon)

Continue Your Journey with Joey Yap's Books

Feng Shui For Homebuyers - Exterior (English & Chinese versions)

Best selling Author and international Feng Shui Consultant, Joey Yap, will guide you on the various important features in your external environment that have a bearing on the Feng Shui of your home. For homeowners, those looking to build their own home or even investors who are looking to apply Feng Shui to their homes, this book provides valuable information from the classical Feng Shui theories and applications.

This book will assist you in screening and eliminating unsuitable options with negative FSQ (Feng Shui Quotient) should you acquire your own land or if you are purchasing a newly built home. It will also help you in determining which plot of land to select and which to avoid when purchasing an empty parcel of land.

Feng Shui for Homebuyers - Interior (English & Chinese versions)

A book every homeowner or potential house buyer should have. The Feng Shui for Homebuyers (Interior) is an informative reference book and invaluable guide written by best selling Author and international Feng Shui Consultant, Joey Yap.

This book provides answers to the important questions of what really does matter when looking at the internal Feng Shui of a home or office. It teaches you how to analyze your home or office floor plans and how to improve their Feng Shui. It will answer all your questions about the positive and negative flow of Qi within your home and ways to utilize them to your maximum benefit.

Providing you with a guide to calculating your Life Gua and House Gua to fine-tune your Feng Shui within your property, Joey Yap focuses on practical, easily applicable ideas on what you can implement internally in a property.

Feng Shui for Apartment Buyers - Home Owners

Finding a good apartment or condominium is never an easy task but who do you ensure that is also has good Feng Shui? And how exactly do you apply Feng Shui to an apartment or condominium or high-rise residence?

These questions and more are answered by renowned Feng Shui Consultant and Master Trainer Joey Yap in **Feng Shui for Apartment Buyers - Home Owners**. Joey answers the key questions about Feng Shui and apartments, then guides you through the bare basics like taking a direction and super-imposing a Flying Stars chart onto a floor plan. Joey also walks you through the process of finding an apartment with favorable Feng Shui, sharing with you some of the key methods and techniques that are employed by professional Feng Shui consultants in assesing apartment Feng Shui.

In his trademark straight-to-the-point manner, Joey shares with you the Feng Shui do's and dont's when it comes to finding an apartment with favorable Feng Shui and which is conducive for home living.

The Ten Thousand Year Calendar

The Ten Thousand Year Calendar or 萬年曆 Wan Nian Li is a regular reference book and an invaluable tool used by masters, practitioners and students of Feng Shui, BaZi (Four Pillars of Destiny), Chinese Zi Wei Dou Shu Astrology (Purple Star), Yi Jing (I-Ching) and Date Selection specialists.

JOEY YAP's *Ten Thousand Year Calendar* provides the Gregorian (Western) dates converted into both the Chinese Solar and Lunar calendar in both the English and Chinese language.

It also includes a comprehensive set of key Feng Shui and Chinese Astrology charts and references, including Xuan Kong Nine Palace Flying Star Charts, Monthly and Daily Flying Stars, Water Dragon Formulas Reference Charts, Zi Wei Dou Shu (Purple Star) Astrology Reference Charts, BaZi (Four Pillars of Destiny) Heavenly Stems, Earthly Branches and all other related reference tables for Chinese Metaphysical Studies.

Continue Your Journey with Joey Yap's Books

Stories and Lessons on Feng Shui (English & Chinese versions)

Stories and Lessons on Feng Shui is a compilation of essays and stories written by leading Feng Shui and Chinese Astrology trainer and consultant Joey Yap about Feng Shui and Chinese Astrology.

In this heart-warming collection of easy to read stories, find out why it's a myth that you should never have Water on the right hand side of your house, the truth behind the infamous 'love' and 'wealth' corners and that the sudden death of a pet fish is really NOT due to bad luck!

More Stories and Lessons on Feng Shui

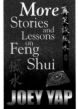

Finally, the long-awaited sequel to *Stories & Lessons on Feng Shui*!

If you've read the best-selling Stories & Lessons on Feng Shui, you won't want to miss this book. And even if you haven't read *Stories & Lessons on Feng Shui*, there's always a time to rev your Feng Shui engine up.

The time is NOW.

And the book? *More Stories & Lessons on Feng Shui* – the 2nd compilation of the most popular articles and columns penned by Joey Yap; **specially featured in national and international publications, magazines and newspapers.**

All in all, *More Stories & Lessons on Feng Shui* is a delightful chronicle of Joey's articles, thoughts and vast experience - as a professional Feng Shui consultant and instructor - that have been purposely refined, edited and expanded upon to make for a light-hearted, interesting yet educational read. And with Feng Shui, BaZi, Mian Xiang and Yi Jing all thrown into this one dish, there's something for everyone...so all you need to serve or accompany *More Stories & Lessons on Feng Shui* with is your favorite cup of tea or coffee!

Even More Stories and Lessons on Feng Shui

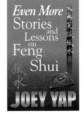

In this third release in the Stories and Lessons series, Joey Yap continues his exploration on the study and practice of Feng Shui in the modern age through a series of essays and personal anecdotes. Debunking superstition, offering simple and understandable "Feng Shui-It-Yourself" tips, and expounding on the history and origins of classical Feng Shui, Joey takes readers on a journey that is always refreshing and exciting.

Besides 'behind-the-scenes' revelations of actual Feng Shui audits, there are also chapters on how beginners can easily and accurately incorporate Feng Shui practice into their lives, as well as travel articles that offer proof that when it comes to Feng Shui, the Qi literally knows no boundaries.

In his trademark lucid and forthright style, Joey covers themes and topics that will strike a chord with all readers who have an interest in Feng Shui.

Mian Xiang - Discover Face Reading (English & Chinese versions)

Need to identify a suitable business partner? How about understanding your staff or superiors better? Or even choosing a suitable spouse? These mind boggling questions can be answered in Joey Yap's introductory book to Face Reading titled *Mian Xiang – Discover Face Reading*. This book will help you discover the hidden secrets in a person's face.

Mian Xiang – Discover Face Reading is comprehensive book on all areas of Face Reading, covering some of the most important facial features, including the forehead, mouth, ears and even the philtrum above your lips. This book will help you analyse not just your Destiny but help you achieve your full potential and achieve life fulfillment.

Continue Your Journey with Joey Yap's Books

BaZi - The Destiny Code (English & Chinese versions)

Leading Chinese Astrology Master Trainer Joey Yap makes it easy to learn how to unlock your Destiny through your BaZi with this book. BaZi or Four Pillars of Destiny is an ancient Chinese science which enables individuals to understand their personality, hidden talents and abilities as well as their luck cycle, simply by examining the information contained within their birth data. *The Destiny Code* is the first book that shows readers how to plot and interpret their own Destiny Charts and lays the foundation for more in-depth BaZi studies. Written in a lively entertaining style, the Destiny Code makes BaZi accessible to the layperson. Within 10 chapters, understand and appreciate more about this astoundingly accurate ancient Chinese Metaphysical science.

BaZi - The Destiny Code Revealed

In this follow up to Joey Yap's best-selling *The Destiny Code*, delve deeper into your own Destiny chart through an understanding of the key elemental relationships that affect the Heavenly Stems and Earthly Branches. Find out how Combinations, Clash, Harm, Destructions and Punishments bring new dimension to a BaZi chart. Complemented by extensive real-life examples, *The Destiny Code Revealed* takes you to the next level of BaZi, showing you how to unlock the Codes of Destiny and to take decisive action at the right time, and capitalise on the opportunities in life.

Xuan Kong: Flying Stars Feng Shui

Xuan Kong Flying Stars Feng Shui is an essential introductory book to the subject of Xuan Kong Fei Xing, a well-known and popular system of Feng Shui, written by International Feng Shui Master Trainer Joey Yap.

In his down-to-earth, entertaining and easy to read style, Joey Yap takes you through the essential basics of Classical Feng Shui, and the key concepts of Xuan Kong Fei Xing (Flying Stars). Learn how to fly the stars, plot a Flying Star chart for your home or office and interpret the stars and star combinations. Find out how to utilise the favourable areas of your home or office for maximum benefit and learn 'tricks of the trade' and 'trade secrets' used by Feng Shui practitioners to enhance and maximise Qi in your home or office.

An essential integral introduction to the subject of Classical Feng Shui and the Flying Stars System of Feng Shui!

Xuan Kong Flying Stars: Structures and Combinations

Delve deeper into Flying Stars through a greater understanding of the 81 Combinations and the influence of the Annual and Monthly Stars on the Base, Sitting and Facing Stars in this 2nd book in the Xuan Kong Feng Shui series. Learn how Structures like the Combination of 10, Up the Mountain and Down the River, Pearl and Parent String Structures are used to interpret a Flying Star chart.

(Available Soon)

Xuan Kong Flying Stars: Advanced Techniques

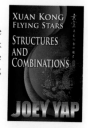

Take your knowledge of Xuan Kong Flying Stars to a higher level and learn how to apply complex techniques and advanced formulas such as Castle Gate Technique, Seven Star Robbery Formation, Advancing the Dragon Formation and Replacement Star technique amongst others. Joey Yap also shows you how to use the Life Palace technique to combine Gua Numbers with Flying Star numbers and utilise the predictive facets of Flying Stars Feng Shui.

(Available Soon)

Annual Releases

Chinese Astrology for 2010

This information-packed annual guide to the Chinese Astrology for 2010 goes way beyond the conventional `animal horoscope' book. To begin with, author Joey Yap includes a personalized outlook for 2010 based on the individual's BaZi Day Pillar (Jia Zi) and a 12-month micro-analysis for each of the 60 Day Pillars – in addition to the annual outlook for all 12 animal signs and the 12-month outlook for each animal sign in 2010. Find out what awaits you in 2010 from the four key aspects of Health, Wealth, Career and Relationships…with Joey Yap's **Chinese Astrology for 2010**!

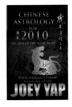

Feng Shui for 2010

Maximize the Qi of the Year of the Metal Tiger for your home and office, with Joey Yap's **Feng Shui for 2010** book. Learn how to tap into the positive sectors of the year, and avoid the negative ones and those with the Annual Afflictions, as well as ascertain how the annual Flying Stars affect your property by comparing them against the Eight Mansions (Ba Zhai) for 2010. Flying Stars enthusiasts will also find this book handy, as it includes the monthly Flying Stars charts for the year, accompanied by detailed commentaries on what sectors to use and avoid – to enable you to optimize your Academic, Relationships and Wealth Luck in 2010.

Weekly Tong Shu Diary 2010

Organize your professional and personal lives with the **Tong Shu Diary 2010**, with a twist… it also allows you to determine the most suitable dates on which you can undertake important activities and endeavors throughout the year! This compact Diary integrates the Chinese Solar and Lunar Calendars with the universal lingua franca of the Gregorian Calendar.

Tong Shu Monthly Planner 2010

Tailor-made for the Feng Shui or BaZi enthusiast in you, or even professional Chinese Metaphysics consultants who want a compact planner with useful information incorporated into it. In the **Tong Shu Monthly Planner 2010**, you will find the auspicious and inauspicious dates for the year marked out for you, alongside the most suitable activities to be undertaken on each day. As a bonus, there is also a reference section containing all the monthly Flying Stars charts and Annual Afflictions for 2010.

Tong Shu Desktop Calendar 2010

Get an instant snapshot of the suitable and unsuitable activities for each day of the Year of the Earth Rat, with the icons displayed on this lightweight Desktop Calendar. Elegantly presenting the details of the Chinese Solar Calendar in the form of the standard Gregorian one, the **Tong Shu Desktop Calendar 2010** is perfect for Chinese Metaphysics enthusiasts and practitioners alike. Whether it a business launching or meeting, ground breaking ceremony, travel or house-moving that you have in mind, this Calendar is designed to fulfill your information needs.

Tong Shu Year Planner 2010

This one-piece Planner presents you all the essential information you need for significant activities or endeavors…with just a quick glance! In a nutshell, it allows you to identify the favorable and unfavorable days, which will in turn enable you to schedule your year's activities so as to make the most of good days, and avoid the ill-effects brought about by inauspicious ones.

Elevate Your Feng Shui Skills With Joey Yap's Home Study Course And Educational DVDs

Xuan Kong Vol.1
An Advanced Feng Shui Home Study Course

Learn the Xuan Kong Flying Star Feng Shui system in just 20 lessons! Joey Yap's specialised notes and course work have been written to enable distance learning without compromising on the breadth or quality of the syllabus. Learn at your own pace with the same material students in a live class would use. The most comprehensive distance learning course on Xuan Kong Flying Star Feng Shui in the market. Xuan Kong Flying Star Vol.1 comes complete with a special binder for all your course notes.

Feng Shui for Period 8 - (DVD)

Don't miss the Feng Shui Event of the next 20 years! Catch Joey Yap LIVE and find out just what Period 8 is all about. This DVD boxed set zips you through the fundamentals of Feng Shui and the impact of this important change in the Feng Shui calendar. Joey's entertaining, conversational style walks you through the key changes that Period 8 will bring and how to tap into Wealth Qi and Good Feng Shui for the next 20 years.

Xuan Kong Flying Stars Beginners Workshop - (DVD)

Take a front row seat in Joey Yap's Xuan Kong Flying Stars workshop with this unique LIVE RECORDING of Joey Yap's Xuan Kong Flying Stars Feng Shui workshop, attended by over 500 people. This DVD program provides an effective and quick introduction of Xuan Kong Feng Shui essentials for those who are just starting out in their study of classical Feng Shui. Learn to plot your own Flying Star chart in just 3 hours. Learn 'trade secret' methods, remedies and cures for Flying Stars Feng Shui. This boxed set contains 3 DVDs and 1 workbook with notes and charts for reference.

BaZi Four Pillars of Destiny Beginners Workshop - (DVD)

Ever wondered what Destiny has in store for you? Or curious to know how you can learn more about your personality and inner talents? BaZi or Four Pillars of Destiny is an ancient Chinese science that enables us to understand a person's hidden talent, inner potential, personality, health and wealth luck from just their birth data. This specially compiled DVD set of Joey Yap's BaZi Beginners Workshop provides a thorough and comprehensive introduction to BaZi. Learn how to read your own chart and understand your own luck cycle. This boxed set contains 3 DVDs and 1 workbook with notes and reference charts.

Interested in learning MORE about Feng Shui? Advance Your Feng Shui Knowledge with the Mastery Academy Courses.

 Feng Shui Mastery Series™
LIVE COURSES (MODULES ONE TO FOUR)

Feng Shui Mastery – Module One
Beginners Course

Designed for students seeking an entry-level intensive program into the study of Feng Shui , Module One is an intensive foundation course that aims not only to provide you with an introduction to Feng Shui theories and formulas and equip you with the skills and judgments to begin practicing and conduct simple Feng Shui audits upon successful completion of the course. Learn all about Forms, Eight Mansions Feng Shui and Flying Star Feng Shui in just one day with a unique, structured learning program that makes learning Feng Shui quick and easy!

Feng Shui Mastery – Module Two
Practitioners Course

Building on the knowledge and foundation in classical Feng Shui theory garnered in M1, M2 provides a more advanced and in-depth understanding of Eight Mansions, Xuan Kong Flying Star and San He and introduces students to theories that are found only in the classical Chinese Feng Shui texts. This 3-Day Intensive course hones analytical and judgment skills, refines Luo Pan (Chinese Feng Shui compass) skills and reveals 'trade secret' remedies. Module Two covers advanced Forms Analysis, San He's Five Ghost Carry Treasure formula, Advanced Eight Mansions and Xuan Kong Flying Stars and equips you with the skills needed to undertake audits and consultations for residences and offices.

Feng Shui Mastery – Module Three
Advanced Practitioners Course

Module Three is designed for Professional Feng Shui Practitioners. Learn advanced topics in Feng Shui and take your skills to a cutting edge level. Be equipped with the knowledge, techniques and confidence to conduct large scale audits (like estate and resort planning). Learn how to apply different systems appropriately to remedy situations or cases deemed inauspicious by one system and reconcile conflicts in different systems of Feng Shui. Gain advanced knowledge of San He (Three Harmony) systems and San Yuan (Three Cycles) systems, advanced Luan Tou (Forms Feng Shui) and specialist Water Formulas.

Feng Shui Mastery – Module Four
Master Course

The graduating course of the Feng Shui Mastery (FSM) Series, this course takes the advanced practitioner to the Master level. Power packed M4 trains students to 'walk the mountains' and identify superior landform, superior grade structures and make qualitative evaluations of landform, structures, Water and Qi and covers advanced and exclusive topics of San He, San Yuan, Xuan Kong, Ba Zhai, Luan Tou (Advanced Forms and Water Formula) Feng Shui. Master Internal, External and Luan Tou (Landform) Feng Shui methodologies to apply Feng Shui at every level and undertake consultations of every scale and magnitude, from houses and apartments to housing estates, townships, shopping malls and commercial districts.

BaZi Mastery – Module One

Intensive Foundation Course

This Intensive One Day Foundation Course provides an introduction to the principles and fundamentals of BaZi (Four Pillars of Destiny) and Destiny Analysis methods such as Ten Gods, Useful God and Strength of Qi. Learn how to plot a BaZi chart and interpret your Destiny and your potential. Master BaZi and learn to capitalize on your strengths, minimize risks and downturns and take charge of your Destiny.

BaZi Mastery – Module Two

Practitioners Course

BaZi Module Two teaches students advanced BaZi analysis techniques and specific analysis methods for relationship luck, health evaluation, wealth potential and career potential. Students will learn to identify BaZi chart structures, sophisticated methods for applying the Ten Gods, and how to read Auxiliary Stars. Students who have completed Module Two will be able to conduct professional BaZi readings.

BaZi Mastery – Module Three

Advanced Practitioners Course

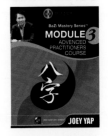

Designed for the BaZi practitioner, learn how to read complex cases and unique events in BaZi charts and perform Big and Small assessments. Discover how to analyze personalities and evaluate talents precisely, as well as special formulas and classical methodologies for BaZi from classics such as Di Tian Sui and Qiong Tong Bao Jian.

BaZi Mastery – Module Four

Master Course in BaZi

The graduating course of the BaZi Mastery Series, this course takes the advanced practitioner to the Masters' level. BaZi M4 focuses on specialized techniques of BaZi reading, unique special structures and advance methods from ancient classical texts. This program includes techniques on date selection and ancient methodologies from the Qiong Tong Bao Jian and Yuan Hai Zi Ping classics.

Xuan Kong Mastery – Module One
Advanced Foundation Course

This course is for the experienced Feng Shui professionals who wish to expand their knowledge and skills in the Xuan Kong system of Feng Shui, covering important foundation methods and techniques from the Wu Chang and Guang Dong lineages of Xuan Kong Feng Shui.

Xuan Kong Mastery – Module Two A
Advanced Xuan Kong Methodologies

Designed for Feng Shui practitioners seeking to specialise in the Xuan Kong system, this program focuses on methods of application and Joey Yap's unique Life Palace and Shifting Palace Methods, as well as methods and techniques from the Wu Chang lineage.

Xuan Kong Mastery – Module Two B
Purple White

Explore in detail and in great depth the star combinations in Xuan Kong. Learn how each different combination reacts or responds in different palaces, under different environmental circumstances and to whom in the property. Learn methods, theories and techniques extracted from ancient classics such as Xuan Kong Mi Zhi, Xuan Kong Fu, Fei Xing Fu and Zi Bai Jue.

Xuan Kong Mastery – Module Three
Advanced Xuan Kong Da Gua

This intensive course focuses solely on the Xuan Kong Da Gua system covering the theories, techniques and methods of application of this unique 64-Hexagram based system of Xuan Kong including Xuan Kong Da Gua for landform analysis.

Walk the Mountains! Learn Feng Shui in a Practical and Hands-on Program

 ## Feng Shui Mastery Excursion Series™ : CHINA

Learn landform (Luan Tou) Feng Shui by walking the mountains and chasing the Dragon's vein in China. This Program takes the students in a study tour to examine notable Feng Shui landmarks, mountains, hills, valleys, ancient palaces, famous mansions, houses and tombs in China. The Excursion is a 'practical' hands-on course where students are shown to perform readings using the formulas they've learnt and to recognize and read Feng Shui Landform (Luan Tou) formations.

Read about China Excursion here:
http://www.masteryacademy.com/Education/schoolfengshui/fengshuimasteryexcursion.asp

Mian Xiang Mastery Series™
LIVE COURSES (MODULES ONE AND TWO)

Mian Xiang Mastery – Module One
Basic Face Reading

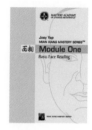

A person's face is their fortune – learn more about the ancient Chinese art of Face Reading. In just one day, be equipped with techniques and skills to read a person's face and ascertain their character, luck, wealth and relationship luck.

Mian Xiang Mastery – Module Two
Practical Face Reading

Mian Xiang Module Two covers face reading techniques extracted from the ancient classics Shen Xiang Quan Pian and Shen Xiang Tie Guan Dau. Gain a greater depth and understanding of Mian Xiang and learn to recognize key structures and characteristics in a person's face.

Yi Jing Mastery Series™
LIVE COURSES (MODULES ONE AND TWO)

Yi Jing Mastery – Module One
Traditional Yi Jing

'Yi', relates to change. Change is the only constant in life and the universe, without exception to this rule. The Yi Jing is hence popularly referred to as the Book or Classic of Change. Discoursed in the language of Yin and Yang, the Yi Jing is one of the oldest Chinese classical texts surviving today. With Traditional Yi Jing, learnn how this Classic is used to divine the outcomes of virtually every facet of life; from your relationships to seeking an answer to the issues you may face in your daily life.

Yi Jing Mastery – Module Two
Plum Blossom Numerology

Shao Yong, widely regarded as one of the greatest scholars of the Sung Dynasty, developed Mei Hua Yi Shu (Plum Blossom Numerology) as a more advanced means for divination purpose using the Yi Jing. In Plum Blossom Numerology, the results of a hexagram are interpreted by referring to the Gua meanings, where the interaction and relationship between the five elements, stems, branches and time are equally taken into consideration. This divination method, properly applied, allows us to make proper decisions whenever we find ourselves in a predicament.

Ze Ri Mastery Series™
LIVE COURSES (MODULES ONE AND TWO)

Ze Ri Mastery Series Module 1
Personal and Feng Shui Date Selection

The Mastery Academy's Date Selection Mastery Series Module 1 is specifically structured to provide novice students with an exciting introduction to the Art of Date Selection. Learn the rudiments and tenets of this intriguing metaphysical science. What makes a good date, and what makes a bad date? What dates are suitable for which activities, and what dates simply aren't? And of course, the mother of all questions: WHY aren't all dates created equal. All in only one Module – Module 1!

Ze Ri Mastery Series Module 2
Xuan Kong Da Gua Date Selection

In Module 2, discover advanced Date Selection techniques that will take your knowledge of this Art to a level equivalent to that of a professional's! This is the Module where Date Selection infuses knowledge of the ancient metaphysical science of Feng Shui and BaZi (Chinese Astrology, or Four Pillars of Destiny). Feng Shui, as a means of maximizing Human Luck (i.e. our luck on Earth), is often quoted as the cure to BaZi, which allows us to decipher our Heaven (i.e. inherent) Luck. And one of the most potent ways of making the most of what life has to offer us is to understand our Destiny, know how we can use the natural energies of our environment for our environments and MOST importantly, WHEN we should use these energies and for WHAT endeavors!

You will learn specific methods on how to select suitable dates, tailored to specific activities and events. More importantly, you will also be taught how to suit dates to a person's BaZi (Chinese Astrology, or Four Pillars of Destiny), in order to maximize his or her strengths, and allow this person to surmount any challenges that lie in wait. Add in the factor of `place', and you would have satisfied the notion of `doing the right thing, at the right time and in the right place'! A basic knowledge of BaZi and Feng Shui will come in handy in this Module, although these are not pre-requisites to successfully undergo Module 2.

Feng Shui for Life

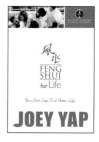

Feng Shui for life is a 5-day course designed for the Feng Shui beginner to learn how to apply practical Feng Shui in day-to-day living. It is a culmination of powerful tools and techniques that allows you to gain quick proficiency in Classical Feng Shui. Discover quick tips on analysing your own BaZi, how to apply Feng Shui solutions for your own home, how to select auspicious dates for important activities, as well as simple and useful Face Reading techniques and practical Water Formulas. This is a complete beginner's course that is suitable for anyone with an interest in applying practical, real-world Feng Shui for life! Enhance every aspect of your life – your health, wealth, and relationships – using these easy-to-apply Classical Feng Shui methods.

Mastery Academy courses are conducted around the world. Find out when will Joey Yap be in your area by visiting **www.masteryacademy.com** or call our office at **+603-2284 8080.**